Your
Financial Edge

HOW TO TAKE THE CURVES IN SHIFTING FINANCIAL MARKETS AND KEEP YOUR PORTFOLIO ON TRACK

Paul McCulley
Jonathan Fuerbringer

John Wiley & Sons, Inc.

Published by John Wiley & Sons, Inc., Hoboken, New Jersey.
Published simultaneously in Canada.

Wiley Bicentennial Logo: Richard J. Pacifico.

For general information on our other products and services or for technical support, please contact our Customer Care Department within the United States at (800) 762-2974, outside the United States at (317) 572-3993 or fax (317) 572-4002.

Wiley also publishes its books in a variety of electronic formats. Some content that appears in print may not be available in electronic books. For more information about Wiley products, visit our web site at www.wiley.com.

Library of Congress Cataloging-in-Publication Data:

McCulley, Paul, 1957–
    Your financial edge : how to take the curves in shifting financial
markets and keep your portfolio on track / Paul McCulley and Jonathan
Fuerbringer.
        p.   cm.
    "Published simultaneously in Canada."
    Includes bibliographical references and index.
    ISBN 978-0-470-04359-2 (cloth)
    1. Portfolio management.   2. Investment analysis.   3. Stock price
forecasting.   4. Investments.   I. Fuerbringer, Jonathan, 1945–.   II. Title.
    HG4529.5.M384   2007
    322.6—dc22   2007003310

Printed in the United States of America.

10 9 8 7 6 5 4 3 2 1

For Everett and Susie McCulley

For Johanna McGeary and the three granddaughters,
Leila Stark, Charlie Fuerbringer, and Siena Stark

Contents

Acknowledgments

Books don't just happen, even when you've been writing all your career, with a huge body of essays over a long period of time in the hopper. A book requires both inspiration and perspiration.

Many have inspired me, but none more than Mohamed El-Erian, Bill Gross, Peter Bernstein, and Bill Miller. Thank you, gentlemen, for believing in me professionally and supporting me personally. Your wise counsel and caring words mean the world to me.

The perspiration for this endeavor came from many sources, with the largest quotient from my co-author, Jonathan Fuerbringer. I had known and respected Jonathan professionally for many years before we took up this project. As it has unfolded, my admiration for Jonathan has been in a powerful bull market. I'm now proud to call him not just my professional partner in crime, but also my dear friend. Thank you, Jonathan, for never letting me quit, when the pain of other exigencies in my life tempted me.

Let me also offer huge thanks to Jim Pankovich, the best executive assistant in the world, who can finish my sentences, even when I cannot.

Kudos, too, for yeo-person statistical work by Vineer Bhansali, Lisa Kim, Steve Schulist, and Craig Bourne.

Special thanks, and love, to my ex-wife, Karen, who tolerated my idiosyncrasies for 17 years, with grace and dignity, while being an awesome mom to our son, Jonathan.

And finally, hugs of appreciation to Saumil Parikh, one of the special ones, of whom only a few grace our lives, both professionally and personally, who is as a second son to me.

—Paul McCulley

This book started with a phone call from Paul McCulley. I was at my desk at *The New York Times* on a calm day in the markets, or both of us would have been too busy to talk.

Paul had an idea. He wanted to do a book based on the "Fed Focus" columns he had written since 1999 at PIMCO, the fixed-income powerhouse headquartered in Newport Beach, California. I did not bite. But Paul persisted, sending me every column he had written. And I began to think he had a good idea as I worked out what kind of book we could do. I also realized that this was a special opportunity—a chance to make good use of all I had learned over a long journalistic career about financial markets and, at the same time, take me away from them for a while. So I thank Paul for asking me to be his co-author, for giving me a pretty free hand, and for the challenge of doing something new. Without his persistence and enthusiasm, this book would not have happened.

Also at PIMCO, thanks to Jim Pankovich, who was the traffic cop between the co-authors. Vineer Bhansali, Lisa Kim, Steve Schulist, and Craig Bourne all helped enormously with their research, numbers crunching, graphic design, and willingness to explain.

At *The New York Times*, thanks to all the good friends who have taught me so much over the years—and whom I missed during my year writing this book. And thanks to Ray Bonner and Jane Perlez, old friends and colleagues, who allowed Johanna and me to make their apartment in Notting Hill our temporary London home.

In the world of finance, there are many who answered my questions, helped me with information, checked my thinking, and gave me some quotes. You all know who you are and I thank you. Thanks also to the data people who fielded my many inquiries, including Robert Adler, Alexa Auerbach, Dorsey Horowitz, Gloria Kim, and Howard Silverblatt. Also thanks to Gary Kleiman, a longtime voice in my ear on emerging markets, who reviewed parts of this book.

At John Wiley & Sons, thanks to Debra Englander, who helped turn an original idea into a publishable one, and Greg Friedman, who put up with every question I threw at him.

I could not have written this book without the counsel of Diana Henriques, another colleague from *The New York Times*, who worked with me from beginning to end on this project, reading, supporting, and guiding all the way.

Finally, and always, I thank Johanna McGeary, my wife. I would not have attempted this book without her behind me. Her love and support—and her ability to make such a wonderful home in London so quickly—all made this book better and life while doing it enjoyable. Thanks and thanks, again.

—Jonathan Fuerbringer

Introduction

The investing environment has changed dramatically in the past 10 years: from taken-for-granted, double-digit annual returns in stocks to double-digit losses and, now, gains that are not even half of what they used to be; from a bubble-fueled mania that led to a complete disregard for fundamental values to the painful aftermath of the bursting of the stock bubble and, maybe, the painful aftermath of the bursting of a second bubble, in housing; from the expectation that you can retire early—and rich—to the fear that you cannot retire at all—and certainly not rich.

On the positive side, the battle against inflation, which began in 1979, has been won, bringing with it all the benefits that come with price stability. But there is even a downside for investors to that victory. With very low inflation the threat to the economy becomes deflation. And with stable prices, speculators are happier and market bubbles are more likely.

Coping with just these changes—and threats—would be enough for any investor. But there are more to come, even as millions of Americans struggle just to earn back what they lost in the first few years of the new century.

There is the next economic downturn, which, with inflation in check, could threaten to tip the country into a bout of deflation, a malady that sent Japan's economy into a 1990s tailspin that has only recently begun to level off.

There are the twin deficits—the current account deficit and the federal budget deficit. The current account deficit is the total of the "borrowing" from abroad Americans have done to buy all they have wanted. At more than $800 billion, the current account deficit is the largest it has ever been. Its unwinding could, at its worst, push up interest rates, send the value of the dollar down sharply, and trigger another economic downturn.

The federal budget deficit is, quite simply, the gap between the promises that the president, the Congress, and the two political parties have made to the people—and their unwillingness to pay the cost of keeping those promises. The budget deficit is not a big problem now, and the official projections for the next 10 years make everything look okay because they show the red ink evaporating. But those rosy projections assumed the expiration, or sunsetting, of President George W. Bush's two big tax cuts. With the current state of Washington gridlock, it looks like it will be difficult to find the blend of tax increases and spending cuts that would turn those rosy deficit projections into reality. And when Social Security can no longer pay for its annual benefits with its payroll tax, which is projected to happen in 2019,[1] the projected deficit for future years will expand rapidly. At that point the federal budget deficit could become disruptive, leading to much higher interest rates than the nation would otherwise experience and much slower economic growth than it might otherwise enjoy.

Then there is China. With apologies to Chico Escuela, it's easy to laugh when the fictional Hispanic baseball player parodied on *Saturday Night Live* observes repeatedly that "basebal bin berra, berra good to me." Well, for most Americans, the punch line would have to be "China bin berra, berra good to me." But it will be no laughing matter when China stops being berra, berra good to us.

China, like many of the other emerging market countries in the world, has been a big contributor to America's successful fight to check inflation. Americans have paid less for the goods from emerging markets, which means prices here have not risen as much as they might have. Despite all the criticism of China for taking away American jobs and competing unfairly for market share, millions of Americans have benefited from lower prices and the victory over inflation.

But that will change as China's economy develops, as its workers get paid more, and as it starts to unwind and reverse a currency policy that has been very helpful to the United States. How much disruption that will cause is debatable, but the unraveling of this special relationship could push both interest rates and prices higher in the United States.

Your Financial Edge is aimed at helping the individual investor—the Main Street investor—deal with these and other important changes in the investing environment:

- A world of lower returns on stocks and bonds, in part because inflation has been contained. In fact, the steady battle to tame inflation in the past three decades provided a better earnings environment for investors than they will find in the post-battle environment of contained inflation.

- A world where globalization continues at full pace and the dollar is not king.

- A world where your best market will not be on Wall Street but in emerging market countries abroad.

- A world where returns will depend a lot more on the skills of professional investment managers, like those running mutual funds, because more investing will need to be done abroad, in environments unfamiliar to do-it-yourself investors.

- A world where diversification into bonds and commodity investments is as important as diversification into markets abroad.

- A world where investors will be living longer, and confronting the need to get better returns so they can build a bigger nest egg to make their savings last longer. Many may have to do this without the safety net of all or part of the pension that was promised to them by their employers and, most likely, with less help than they hoped to get from Social Security.

Your Financial Edge pulls together the thinking on investing and the investing environment of Paul McCulley, a money manager and Federal Reserve watcher at Pacific Investment Management

Company LLC (PIMCO), one of the nation's most prestigious mutual fund companies, and Jonathan Fuerbringer, a financial writer at *The New York Times* for 24 years.

In *Your Financial Edge*, we argue that Main Street investors simply must take more risk if they want to do well in the years ahead. This increased level of risk will certainly make some investors uncomfortable. But the U.S. stock market is struggling to produce modest returns, returns that are miles away from the big double-digit gains of the late 1990s. And even a return to the historic norms for the domestic market means that the average gains will stay in single-digit territory. As for the bond market, returns from safe Treasury securities have dipped in recent years to levels not seen since the 1950s. And even now, after the Federal Reserve has pushed interest rates higher since 2004, the yield on Treasury securities is still well below what used to be normal.

So investors, especially those who have retired or are about to, have no alternative. While Treasury securities are still a haven for investors because of their low risk of loss or default, they may not be a safe harbor for those who want an adequate retirement income. Without adding more risk to your portfolio—even if it is heavily invested in U.S. stocks—your investment earnings could just be too low to live on, even if you have done a good job of saving for retirement.

Adding more than what has been considered normal or average risk to your portfolio may become so de rigueur that Wall Street will adjust all its risk-measuring devices to make it appear that no more than normally needed risk is being taken, even if many investors say they have no stomach for it. (So-called sophisticated investors are already doing this, using hedge funds, complex securities called derivatives, and other similar tools.)

Without a doubt, this shift toward greater risk will be difficult for many investors, leading to some sleepless nights for many of us. And there are some sound reasons to worry.

It has become harder to offset higher risk in your domestic portfolio by diversifying into foreign markets. Once upon a time, those markets tended to move at their own pace, in their own directions, acting as a counterbalance to the pace and direction of the market at home. But as we will point out, too many foreign stock markets abroad now are moving in line with Wall Street, going up and down at the same time. It is especially disturbing that this so-called correlation between stock markets in the United States and stock markets abroad, while pronounced when markets are climbing, is even stronger when the U.S. stock market is falling.

Adding to the discomfort will be the strange and unfamiliar markets that investors will have to explore to increase their returns—emerging markets abroad and corporate and junk bond markets at home.

Finally, investors will have to take on some currency risk, expecting that the value of the dollar will fall over time against the world's other major and minor currencies. If that happens, foreign gains will translate into even larger profits when they are brought home and converted into dollars.

What we want to do with this book is make this addition of risk as understandable and palatable as possible. We show you how low your current risk level probably is, and outline intelligent ways to raise it. We also show you how to take other steps to diversify your portfolio, an essential part of managing your risks.

Then, we look at risk from another perspective—the what-if perspective—as we examine what can go wrong in the current investing environment.

For example, we explore the threat of those twin deficits. We think the current account deficit, which must be reduced at some point, can be slimmed down without too much damage. But that assumes that there is no threat of protectionism and that the rest of the world, which has been happy to keep lending to the United States, does not unexpectedly turn off the credit spigot.

We explain why China has had a close enough economic relationship with the U.S. economy and its monetary policy to almost justify calling it the 51st state. We think this relationship is a bulwark against a messy resolution of the problem with the current account deficit. But an orderly reduction in the current account deficit and the avoidance of a sudden break with China still will not mean that American investors will escape any pain from the rebalancing of the nation's current account deficit. A reduction in this deficit still will mean a weaker dollar, higher interest rates, and higher consumer prices.

We also look into what we think is the biggest threat to the economy and American investors: the next economic downturn, the next recession. There are two reasons a slump would be so scary. One is that a slowdown, which can put downward pressure on prices and inflation, could mean that deflation will become a threat. The other is that it might be more difficult than usual for the Federal Reserve, the nation's central bank, to restart the economy the next time it stutters because the housing market will be so battered.

Market bubbles are also on our list of the difficulties that investors will have to grapple with in the years ahead. Newborn bubbles are not bad, of course. They are just strong trends, surges in consensus opinion that can be a great thing for investors who are quick enough to take advantage of them. But no investor who lived through the end of the preceding century and the beginning of this one needs a lesson in the damage bubbles can do when they blow up and then burst.

What may surprise you is that one of the reasons there will certainly be future bubbles is that the Federal Reserve has done such a good job of taming inflation and stabilizing the economy. That environment, as it happens, is a perfect petri dish for the kind of speculation that gives rise to financial bubbles. That's one of the unexpected downsides of the victory over inflation.

The Federal Reserve's success on inflation is also a reason that returns have shrunk in both the stock and bond markets. As the Fed was winning the fight against inflation, it provided a one-time opportunity for big returns in the bond market as interest rates adjusted to new lower levels. There were even bigger returns in the stock market as the prospect of declining inflation raised the value of future equity earnings in line with falling interest rates, and then some. But now both these markets are assuming that inflation will be stable, with real rates and price-earnings (P/E) multiples reflecting that stability. And you do not get to go to heaven twice for winning the war against inflation—the "peace dividend" is paid just once, as the victory occurs, not year after year in its aftermath.

The governors of the Federal Reserve Board and the presidents of the 12 regional Federal Reserve banks now have to shoulder the task of getting us through the next recession without a deflationary spiral, and through the next bubble without too much damage to the financial system and the economy. Later in this book, we look at their ability to do this and propose a tool for managing monetary policy that would be helpful to both investors and the policy makers at the nation's central bank.

While it is easier to read the intentions of Federal Reserve policy makers than it was several decades ago, their statements and speeches can still be confusing, leading investors to make mistakes. We will tell investors how to figure out what Federal Reserve policy makers are doing as they are doing it, and we roll out our favorite leading indicator of Fed policy. But one old adage is still true—do not bet against the Fed. And do not doubt the policy makers' anti-inflation commitment. They would still rather risk a recession than see a resurgence in inflation.

All of these insights and explanations should help everyday investors navigate the difficult curves—and the easier straightaways—on their financial highways. You must not be distracted from good sense on the straightaways, as millions of investors were in the late 1990s stock market. And you need to be increasingly careful on the curves, because they are going to become sharper and tighter in the years ahead.

At the end of the book, we discuss adjusting your portfolio for the changed investing environment. We go into detail about the markets where investors can take on more risk, especially emerging markets. We look at what investors can do when the Federal Reserve is tightening and when the Fed is easing. We talk about betting on a longer-term dollar decline.

We also take a side trip into the world of mutual funds to

look at the consequences of being right and of being wrong as a money manager—and we illustrate how being right or wrong can make a difference of billions of dollars very quickly. And we show what groupthink did to the best call on interest rates that McCulley has ever made at PIMCO. We will also take a peek at McCulley's portfolio—a look that will show that he is much more of a Main Street investor than you might think. For years, in fact, his most exotic investment was his home! McCulley will also lay out what he is doing with his own money in two investing situations, one a plan for his son and the other the investments for his foundation. And we offer a primer on some of the big—and small—thoughts that drive markets.

McCulley's insights are based on years of economic forecasting and money management at PIMCO. Since September of 1999, he has expressed his views on monetary policy, markets, and economic thought in his "Fed Focus" column, which was recently renamed "Global Central Bank Focus."

At *The New York Times*, Jonathan Fuerbringer was a financial columnist and wrote extensively about economic policy, the Federal Reserve, and stocks, bonds, commodities, and currencies.

McCulley is Mr. Inside: the trained economist who can crunch the numbers and the theories. He understands how interest rates and stocks interact. He can explain clearly the risks of a falling dollar and what to do about it. He knows what it means for investors to have China looming on their economic horizon. Fuerbringer is Mr. Outside: the experienced commentator on markets, accustomed to looking at them from an investor's point of view. He knows the potential pitfalls for individual investors and how to explain good strategies to them.

Many of the ideas in *Your Financial Edge* come from McCulley's columns. PIMCO has graciously allowed us to refer to these ideas and use many of the columns in this book.[2] Fuerbringer has written about emerging markets and diversification in *The New York Times*; in stories in the business section; in his column, "Portfolios, Etc."; and in his contribution to the book *The New Rules of Personal Investing*, edited by Allen R. Myerson and published by Times Books in 2002. *The New York Times* and Times Books have graciously allowed him to examine these and other ideas in *Your Financial Edge*.[3]

Obviously, we do not have all the answers. No one does. Like all portfolio managers and journalists who have offered their views on investing, we have been wrong in the past. But we have also been right. And we think our views offer both an intelligent sense of the current and future investing environments and the proper amount of caution.

We cannot make investing less difficult than it is. Even if you are investing for the long term and using well-known mutual fund companies or a smart money manager that you like, you still have to question the advice you get, make your choices, and live with the consequences.

And we are not, like some prognosticators, preparing you for the good time or the bad time we see ahead. We are predicting neither an investing nirvana nor an investing debacle ahead—just curves and straightaways.

1

New Steps

Meet risk. You know what it looks like—a little scary. You know how it makes you feel—queasy. You know what it can do to your portfolio—make it shrink.

Right, right, and wrong. Scary, queasy, yes. But risk does not produce just losses. In fact, based on historical data, it is well proven that adding risk can improve investor returns over time.

So return, which you know and love, has a regular dance partner. And the better they dance together, the better you and your portfolio perform.

You may have been doing only a safe waltz with risk for years, or maybe a little bit jazzier foxtrot. Now it is time to learn some more difficult—and, probably, intimidating—steps: the quickstep or a tango.

Diminishing expectations and a harsher reality are the reasons for this new investor choreography.

Too many people have been expecting the much higher than average returns of the end of the 1990s to carry them through their retirement. The truth is that future returns are unlikely to repeat this performance and could be less than average.

Low inflation makes the return environment for both stocks and bonds less hopeful even when the economy is in fine shape. And recessions—yes, there will be more—will undermine corporate earnings and stock returns even more, while lowering the yield on all types of bonds. Smaller personal portfolios, savaged in the bear market that began in 2000, mean returns have to be higher. And the tampering that is going on with promised corporate pension benefits means there is less of a cushion for millions of investors.

This turn of events is most difficult for those investors near or in retirement. These older investors are traditionally most risk-averse—and have reason to be. But they will be faced with the choice of a lower standard of living or taking more risk.

Older Americans also have to face the fact that they are expected to live a lot longer than their parents. Because of that, those near retirement and even those already retired will have to keep a much bigger portion of stocks in their portfolios than their parents would have. As we will see, this adds risk.

First, let's take a look at expectations and reality.

The 28.6 percent compound annual rate of return for the stock market at the end of the 1990s is a dream now.[1] Those returns were the product, in part, of a revolution in the investing environment as the Federal Reserve, the nation's central bank, conquered inflation and the federal government seemed to get sensible about its own fiscal policies, which led to an all-too-brief period of federal budget surpluses. While the term *new economy* may have fallen into disrepute, the sometimes baffling surge in worker productivity that characterized this period was also behind the rise in equities, as was more than 18 years of economic growth, interrupted by just one recession.

Now the stock market should return to its slower, longer-term pace of appreciation, which you can see in Table 1.1. The market crash that began in 2000 has already gotten this process well un-

TABLE 1.1 Keeping Up with History?

	Total Return	Total Real Return
1926–2006	10.4%	7.2%
1946–2006	11.5%	7.2%
1946–1965	13.8%	10.7%
1966–1981	6.0%	–1.0%
1982–1999	18.5%	14.8%
1995–1999	28.6%	25.6%
1982–2006	13.4%	10.0%

Returning to the historic pace of stock returns means a big decline from the pace of the 1990s. Total returns and real total returns, adjusted for inflation, at compound annual rates.
Source: Ibbotson Associates. Data from Standard & Poor's.

der way. The compound annual rate of total return, including dividends, for the Standard & Poor's 500 stock index in the seven years since 2000 is just 1.1 percent, despite double-digit gains in 2003, 2004, and 2006.

One reason for this belief is what economists call mean reversion, which says that over time the return from the stock market will revert to its historical trend. So if you have had a period when market performance was well above its long-term trend—like the 18.5 percent compound annual pace from 1982 through 1999 or the 28.6 percent run from 1995 through 1999—then a period of subtrend growth is due. This means that returns should move below their long-term average.

So what should that be? The compound annual rate of return for stocks from 1946 through 2006 is 11.5 percent, with the after-inflation or real return at 7.2 percent. So investors may be faced not with just half the returns from the 1990s stock bubble, but less than half.

Another reason for thinking stock market returns will be lower is the valuation of the equity market. Stocks in the closely watched S&P 500 stock index are still a little expensive historically, even after the collapse that began in 2000. As of the end of

2006, the price-to-earnings ratio for the S&P 500 stock index was 17.4, according to Standard & Poor's. That is above the P/E average of 16.1 since World War II, although it is well below its peak of 46.5 for 2001.

The P/E ratio on the Dow Jones Wilshire 5000 index, which includes all stocks of companies based in the United States, was 19.5 at the end of 2006, according to Wilshire Associates, just above its annual average of 19.3 since 1979. So valuations do not have that far to rise before they could become a worry.

Jeremy J. Siegel, the Russell E. Palmer Professor of Finance at the Wharton School of the University of Pennsylvania and the author of the influential book *Stocks for the Long Run*, expects the real, or after-inflation, compound annual rate of total return to fall to 6 percent, a full percentage point below the real return since World War II and less than half the real compound annual rate of return of 14.8 percent from 1982 through 1999. And he acknowledged in an e-mail interview that the real return could fall lower.

In dollars, this downshift in returns since the 1990s means that a portfolio invested all in stocks would have a 8.5 percent nominal return, which is Siegel's 6 percent prediction for the after-inflation return, with 2.5 percentage points of inflation added on. It would take eight and a half years for the portfolio to double in size. At 6.5 percent, including inflation, a much more pessimistic assumption, the portfolio would take 11 years to double in size.

That is a portfolio slowdown. Using the 18.5 percent compound annual total return from 1982 through 1999, that portfolio invested in stocks would double in size in just over four years. A 1990s portfolio doubled in less than three years.

Another reason to take more risk is that many investors have to make do with less. Investor portfolios that were stuffed with technology and telecommunications stocks have not recovered from the losses suffered when the bubble popped.

Only the Dow Jones Industrial Average, the narrowest of the popular stock market barometers, had surpassed its pre-crash closing high by the end of 2006. The Dow Jones Wilshire 5000 was still 3.3 percent below its all-time high at the end of 2006, while the S&P 500 stock index was 7.1 percent below its closing high. The technology-heavy NASDAQ Composite index was a staggering 52.2 percent below its high.

Many Americans also have lost or are threatened with losing the pensions they have counted on from their companies. Others are facing freezes that will reduce the expected value of their retirement benefits. Among the big-name companies that announced the freezing of their benefits in 2006 alone were IBM, Alcoa, Northwest Airlines, and Sprint Nextel. And it is possible that state, county, and municipal employees could face threats to their pensions similar to those now faced by government workers in San Diego.[2]

Outside of the stock market, returns are even worse. In fact, the traditional safe harbor for millions of investors, the U.S. Treasury securities market, may still be safe but it is not a particularly profitable place to put one's money or hopes for retirement.

The yields on Treasury securities were at their lowest in almost half a century in 2003 and could be headed even lower in the future. Even with a rise in interest rates that began in the summer of 2004, the Treasury's 10-year note was yielding only 4.71 percent at the end of 2006, which means that a Treasury portfolio would take more than 15 years to double in size. That yield is uncomfortably lower than the five-year average of 5.95 percent through 2000, after which rates fell sharply. That average would have doubled the size of a portfolio in 12 years.

But unless there is a revival of inflation, it is unlikely that rates will get near that average again for any length of time. In fact, it is more likely that these interest rates will go even lower, making the safe harbor of the Treasury market an unsafe place for investors to be in if they are in any way worried about the size of their returns.

Adding to this threat of lower interest rates in the Treasury and other fixed-income markets is the expectation of recessions in the years ahead. When they happen, the slowing of growth will push interest rates even lower and bring down prices and the inflation rate.

At that point, the Federal Reserve will be faced with two problems. One will be to prevent the economic slowdown from deepening. The other—and more serious—problem will be to prevent a slowing in the rate of inflation, which is called disinflation, from turning into deflation, an actual decline in prices.

In the most recent recession, which ended in November of 2001, Federal Reserve policy makers were open about the threat of deflation as they pushed Treasury interest rates lower and lower. Their short-term interest rate target, which is the central bank's main tool for steering the course of the economy, got down to 1 percent in June of 2003 and stayed there for a year. It is likely that in the next recession, this rate will have to go below 1 percent.

During the time that the federal funds rate was at 1 percent, the yield on the Treasury's 10-year note fell as low as 3.13 percent in June of 2003, the lowest yield on a 10-year maturity since July of 1958, based on Federal Reserve interest rate data.

The money managers at PIMCO, the big bond mutual fund company where McCulley works, are predicting that the yield on the Treasury's 30-year bond, which was revived by the government in 2006, could fall below 4 percent in the next three to five years. It was at 4.81 percent at the end of 2006. How tempting is it to tie up your money for 30 years for an annual return of 3.5 percent? You'll just have to look elsewhere and try a new dance step with the risk in your portfolio.

The scramble for better returns by taking on more risk has been under way for a while by many big institutional investors and mutual fund money managers. And it has already had perverse results for investors who have been waiting to embrace their new partner for return. As more and more people take on a little bit more risk to better their returns, the gain for that added risk declines for those not on the dance floor.

If more and more investors are willing to buy riskier investments, for example moving even cautiously from a portfolio stashed in the Treasury market to one filled with investment-grade corporate bonds, that new demand bids up the price for those corporate bonds. Prices and yields move in opposite directions, so when investors pay a higher price for these corporate bonds they get a lower yield. As prices of riskier assets rise, the return for that added risk decreases.

This willingness to take on added risk is one of the reasons that longer-term interest rates remained unexpectedly low in 2004, 2005, and 2006, even as the Federal Reserve raised its short-term interest rate target, the federal funds rate on overnight loans. After the central bank had increased its target by 4.25 percentage points, from 1 percent to 5.25 percent, the yield on the Treasury's 10-year note at the end of 2006 was virtually at the 4.70 percent level of June 2004, when the Federal Reserve began that round of interest rate increases. The yield on the 10-year note did not get above 5 percent until April of 2006, the first time in four years, but stayed there for only four months.

In other words, we are in the midst of a risk squeeze, where investors will get less for more risk. So it is likely that many investors, in order to meet their investment and savings goals, will have to take on what is now considered above-average risk just to get an average return, or substantial risk to get an above-average return.

The most cautious investors, whether they like it or not, will not have the luxury of putting much of their money into the traditional safe harbor of the Treasury market and earning enough to live on.

BLAME STABILITY

The reason investors have to get to know risk better, despite the potential discomfort, is that we got what we wished for—an economy with inflation in check.

The long secular battle against inflation began with the appointment of Paul A. Volcker as chairman of the Federal Reserve in 1979 by President Jimmy Carter, and was won, for now, during Alan Greenspan's more than 18 years at the helm of the nation's central bank. He retired at the end of January 2006.

All in all, economists agree that while no scheme for managing an economy is perfect, one battle—the battle against inflation—has to be won if there is going to be hope for long-term growth.

But even such a cure-all has its downside. In this case, it is that the roller-coaster ride to lower inflation can be much more profitable for investors than the stable price environment the containment of inflation brings. That is because there is a one-time upward revaluation of the value of assets, like stocks, bonds, and real estate, as inflation in wrung out of the system. And investors have already profited from that.

There is a difference between going to financial heaven and living there. During the journey there is a suspension of the historical relationship between stock prices and earnings that allows equities to generate extraordinary returns. It's akin to suspending the speed limit on an interstate highway. But once the journey is over, stock prices and earnings return to their historical relationship and the expected return for stocks, like the speed limit, falls.

To put it another way, total returns for stocks over the past two decades are irrelevant in considering the merits of stocks for the next two decades.

Now that we are at a level of inflation that is hovering around 2 percent and staying there is the goal of economic policy, there is a smaller chance for an extra boost to asset valuations and above-average profits for investors.

And if anything happens with inflation it is not likely to be good. If there is a rise in inflation, say to 4 percent, that will kill the bond market, sending prices and returns for investors down. Stocks will be undermined by the higher interest rates, and rising inflation will make future corporate profits less attractive. If there is a further decline in inflation, deflation becomes a threat, and the fallout on both stocks and bonds would be even worse.

WHAT TO DO

Younger investors should be taking on the most risk. Other investors should be scaling up their risk level, almost no matter what age they are.

We are not asking you to walk the risk plank. We are not saying that you have to take all your money from a safer place and move it to a riskier place. We do not want you to have nightmares.

But you have to take a first step. Then, over time, you can learn to adjust your portfolio, not only to take on more risk, but also to respond to changes in the market environment.

If you are very conservative, with most of your money in Treasury securities and money-market funds, your first move is to shift money into investment-grade corporate bonds, which have higher yields than Treasury securities and money-market funds. Then you could shift some of your money into stocks, knowing that you intend to keep it there for the long term, at least 10 years.

If you are already much more adventurous and have a lot of your portfolio in stocks, you can add risk by changing your mix of stocks. For example, you can move into smaller company stocks—what are called small-capitalization or small-cap stocks.

A bolder step is to invest abroad. To this end you can add a lot of risk by moving to emerging markets, the growing stock markets in developing nations.

How much do these shifts in risk help you? Let's take a look. Remember that the historical data used here is to give you a way to compare the risk and return trade-offs of the various investment categories we are describing. These compound annual rates of return do not tell you what you will earn in the future. They are only an indication of the difference in returns possible for different levels of risk.

Also remember that we believe that the returns from both the stock market and the bond market will be lower in the years ahead. So these historical returns are even less likely to be repeated.

Risk here is measured by what economists call the standard deviation of annual returns. The higher this number, the riskier the investment because the assets chosen have a wider range of returns, both positive and negative, over time.

In the 81 years through 2006, 30-day Treasury bills have been the safest place to be, as can be seen in Table 1.2. Their risk measure—their standard deviation—is way down at 3.1. These Treasury bills have produced a loss in only one year, in 1938. But their compound annual rate of return over those 81 years is just 3.7 percent, according to Ibbotson Associates, a Morningstar company.[3]

Even a relatively small increase in risk, however, can improve

TABLE 1.2   Getting More Return for More Risk: Where to Find It

	Years Through 2006	Compound Annual Rate of Return	Standard Deviation	Number of Positive Years	Number of Negative Years
S&P 500 stock index	81	10.4%	20.1	58	23
U.S. small-cap stocks	81	12.7%	32.7	57	24
U.S. 30-day Treasury bill	81	3.7%	3.1	80	1
MSCI EAFE Index	37	11.6%	21.9	27	10
Goldman Sachs Commodity Index	37	11.5%	24.1	28	9
Lehman U.S. Aggregate Index	31	8.6%	7.4	29	2
Lehman High-Yield Index	23	9.8%	12.3	19	4
MSCI Emerging Market Index	19	15.2%	33.6	11	8
JPMorgan EMBI Global Index	13	10.9%	14.8	11	2

Source: Ibbotson Associates.
Data from Federal Reserve, Goldman Sachs, JP Morgan, Lehman Brothers, MSCI, Standard & Poor's.

the outlook for returns. A move from the safest corner of the Treasury market to a mix of Treasury securities, from bills to bonds, and the addition of investment-grade corporate bonds and securities backed by mortgages raises the compound annual return over the past 31 years to 8.6 percent. The risk factor is 7.4, more than twice the risk of the safest of the safe, Treasury bills. In those 31 years, there was a loss in only two years.

Your new portfolio would look like the composition of the Lehman Brothers U.S. Aggregate Index,[4] with 40 percent in mortgage-backed and other so-called securitized securities, 25 percent in Treasury securities, almost 20 percent in investment-grade corporate bonds, and 15 percent in other government-related securities, including the so-called agency bonds issued by the likes of Fannie Mae. If you decreased the Treasury portion and just moved the money into corporate bonds, for example, your risk and potential return would rise a little.

With interest rates much lower than they have been and, as we warned early in this chapter, likely to go lower, investors cannot expect to receive the 8.6 percent compound annual return of the past for this portfolio based on the Lehman Aggregate. But this portfolio is still going to be better than just staying in Treasury securities. In the five years through 2006, the compound annual return for a portfolio invested along the lines of the Lehman Aggregate was 5.1 percent, compared to 4.6 percent for a portfolio of just Treasury securities, according to Lehman Brothers. That may not sound like much of a difference, but the Lehman Aggregate portfolio doubles in 14 years, more than a year before the Treasury portfolio.

To get more risk out of the bond market, investors can choose high-yield or so-called junk bonds. These are corporate bonds that are rated below investment grade, which means there is a much greater chance that the company that issued them will default on its payments of principal and interest. But these bonds have become a popular addition to many portfolios because of the much higher potential yields they offer compared to Treasury securities and investment-grade corporate bonds.

In the five years through 2006, the Lehman Brothers High-Yield Index had a compound annual return of 10.2 percent, twice the return from the Lehman Aggregate portfolio over that period. Since 1984, the compound annual return for high-yield bonds has been 9.8 percent, but their risk level is a standard deviation of 12.3, according to Ibbotson Associates, nearly twice that of the Lehman Aggregate portfolio.

But the big jump in risk—and return—is going from bonds into stocks. The compound annual return from the Standard & Poor's 500 stock index over the past 81 years is 10.4 percent,[5] which is quite acceptable. It means that a person's portfolio would take just seven years to double in value, which is a lot faster pace than the bond portfolio offers. While lower stock returns will make portfolio doubling take longer in the years ahead, the potential rate for stocks will still be a lot faster than for bonds.

The price is higher risk, with the standard deviation for the S&P 500 at 20.1, which is more than six times the risk of Treasury bills. And in 23 of the 81 years of history, the S&P 500 had a loss.

To go even further out on the risk plank, investors could choose smaller company stocks. These are companies that you will not find in the Standard & Poor's 500 stock index or in the Dow Jones Industrial Average. They are generally relatively new firms and often do not yet have a steady stream of earnings. Some do well; some do not. Some fail. That adds to their risk, but that is what also makes their potential returns higher. They are called small caps in Wall Street jargon, for small capitalization. A company's capitalization is its stock price times the number of shares outstanding.

The risk barometer for smaller company stocks is at 32.7, more than 10 times that of Treasury bills. And in 24 of the past 81 years, smaller company stocks had a loss. But their compound annual return over those 81 years is 12.7 percent.

The nicest blend of greater risk and bigger returns is in the stock and bond markets outside of the United States. We will be calling this the international part of your portfolio, because that coincides with the terminology in mutual funds, where a fund that is called international invests most of its money outside of the United States. A global mutual fund, in contrast, can invest anywhere, which means it could have most of its money in the United States, despite the title.

In the developed stock markets abroad—from London to Tokyo—investors have gotten a better compound annual return than from the Standard & Poor's 500 stock index, based on history, but with more risk. Since 1970, the Morgan Stanley Capital International (MSCI) index of foreign developed stock markets, known as the EAFE (Europe, Australasia, Far East) index, has had a compound annual return of 11.6 percent, with a risk measure of 21.9 percent.[6] The return is 1.2 percentage points more than that for the S&P 500, while the risk level is 1.8 points higher.

But the biggest bang for the buck comes from emerging stock markets. Their risk is not much higher than smaller company stocks and they have had a higher return. So you always have to consider both numbers together.

These emerging stock markets are in both the world's well-known, rapidly developing economies, including China, South Korea, India, Brazil, and Russia, and in some less well-known developing economies, including Sri Lanka and Zimbabwe. This is one of the biggest risk shifts most Americans will have to make in the years ahead to increase returns.

Despite their roller-coaster history, emerging stock markets, based on the performance of the MSCI index for these markets, have a risk level that is only slightly higher than small-cap stocks—33.6 compared to 32.7. But the compound annual return for emerging stock markets through 2006 was 15.2 percent, compared to 12.7 percent for small-cap stocks. In a race of two $250,000 portfolios, the emerging market one would be at $2.1 million in 15 years, when the small-cap portfolio would be at $1.5 million.

The bond markets in emerging market countries, which are sort of equivalent to the high-yield or junk bond market in the

United States, also offer a step up in return and risk for willing American investors. Emerging market bonds have had a compound annual return of 10.9 percent since 1994, with a risk level of 14.8, based on JPMorgan's Emerging Markets Bond Index (EMBI) Global.[7]

Because of these risk-return numbers, foreign markets present the best and most diverse place for Americans to take on more risk in their effort to improve their average returns over time.

Outside of stocks and bonds, an investor can consider commodities as another asset class for increasing risk in a portfolio. Since 1970, the return of the Goldman Sachs Commodity Index, which includes gold, oil, wheat, copper, and lean hogs, has had a compound annual return of 11.5 percent, while the standard deviation has been 24.1.[8] This may seem a little far afield for some investors, but, as we will show in Chapter 2, commodities can also be a good diversifying additive to a portfolio that reduces overall risk. And commodities have had an amazing run the past eight years, with a compound annual return of 14.5 percent through 2006.

WHERE YOU ARE

There are investors out there who are already taking the risk we are advocating, and there are people out there who will never have a chance even to think about it. But saying exactly where American investors are on the risk spectrum is difficult.

Overall data from the federal government or from mutual funds gives you a broad picture, an idea of the preference of investors as a whole. But mutual fund data may not reflect the average individual portfolio because many investors have money elsewhere, including in their 401(k) plans, in their banks, in their homes, and in individual stocks and bonds.

This data also cannot reflect the wide possible range of portfolios, from people with very little money at all to those who have millions and can afford hefty fees each year for professionals to tell them what to do.

Still, we need to use these proxies to get a picture of what is going on with risk. And, in its broad reading, this data says that not enough risk is being taken.

American investors' willingness to buy foreign stocks and bonds was the lowest among the six developed economics examined by the International Monetary Fund in 2005, falling well behind the Netherlands, the United Kingdom, and France, and trailing Germany and Japan.[9]

There also has been a decline from the 1999 peak of the total holdings of stocks owned by Americans and a buildup of so-called cash holdings in the past several years, reflecting a fall in the level of overall risk in American portfolios.

The share of stocks in the overall household portfolio fell to 38.1 percent of financial assets in 2005, from 50.3 percent in 1999, according to the latest annual flow of funds data from the Federal Reserve. The fall in the share of stocks in the household portfolio reflected both the decline in value of the stocks and net sales of stocks by investors. At the same time, the sum of household bank deposits and money-market funds rose as a percentage of financial assets, to 15.7 percent from 11.7 percent in 1999. Federal Reserve data through the third quarter of 2006 showed that there had not been a big change in this balance of stocks and cash.

As of the third quarter of 2006, Americans had more than $7.1 trillion in checking accounts, savings accounts, money-market funds, Treasury securities, and savings bonds. That was 17.6 percent of household financial assets and just too much money at work earning the least that it can.

Investor risk appetite is down in some other barometers, as can be seen in Table 1.3. The most recent survey by the Investment Company Institute and the Securities Industry Association on risk showed that 66 percent of those interviewed in 2005 would only take average risk or less in the stock market. That

TABLE 1.3   A Small Retreat on Risk: Willingness of Equity
Investors to Take Financial Risk 1999–2005

	1999	2002	2005
Substantial risk for substantial gain	9%	8%	6%
Above-average risk for above-average gain	31%	24%	28%
Average risk for average gain	48%	51%	49%
Below-average risk for below-average gain	7%	10%	9%
Unwilling to take any risk	6%	7%	8%
Number of respondents	2,299	2,104	2,344

Source: Investment Company Institute/Securities Industry Association.
1999 survey does not add to 100% due to rounding.

was up from 61 percent in 1999, at the height of the bull market.
Those willing to take on above-average or substantial risk—in
exchange for the opportunity to get above-average or substantial
returns—had fallen to 34 percent in 2005, from 40 percent in
1999.[10]

Since we think it will take more than average risk to get what
was considered an average return in the past, this data indicates
that many investors have been moving in the wrong direction on
what they think should be their tolerance for risk.

The mismatch between the extra risk we are advocating and
the risk investors are taking is even greater when investors are 50
or older. In the 50 to 64 age bracket, only 27 percent of investors
were willing to take either above-average or substantial risk to
improve their returns, according to the same survey. And in the
over-65 age group, the percentage of higher-risk investors fell to
18 percent.[11] That meant that 82 percent were taking only average risk or less. Twenty-nine percent would take only below-
average risk or no risk at all, which had to leave many of these
investors depending too much on the measly yields from the U.S.
Treasury market—and at a time when longer life expectancy is
an argument for more stocks and, therefore, more risk when you
are older.

Other measures show that even though the appetite for foreign stocks has grown, investors are still well short of the levels of foreign exposure we think they will need in the years ahead.

Analysts have been recommending for years that foreign stocks should account for somewhere between 25 percent and 40 percent of the stock portion of an investor's portfolio. But as a percentage of all the equities owned by mutual funds, foreign stocks were at 18 percent at the end of 2006,[12] up from 9.4 percent at the end of 1999, according to AMG Data Services, which monitors the flow of money in and out of mutual funds.

William Libby, the director at InterSec Research, a company that focuses on international investing by pension funds, said he thinks that half a stock portfolio should be abroad, for the added risk and potential reward and the fact that more than half the world's stocks are outside the United States. Pension funds, he added, are just about as far behind as mutual fund investors, with only 16.3 percent of their stock portfolios abroad, as of the end of 2005. This underweighting of foreign stocks is not good for investors, because many of the pension funds they will depend on in their retirement are having trouble making the returns they need to guarantee their future pension payments.

In addition to being low on foreign stocks, American investors are way too low on emerging market stocks in their international portfolios. Analysts and financial journalists have always cautioned about going too heavily into emerging markets, where the overall market can jump 60 percent one year and fall 30 percent the next year. Five percent was a recommendation for those with a strong stomach years ago. Now investors need a lot more.

As of the end of 2006, the $153.6 billion in emerging market equity funds added up to just 2.9 percent of the more than $5.3 trillion in all equity funds, according to AMG Data. The percentage of emerging market stocks in the MSCI All Country World Index (ACWI), a compilation of the world's equity markets, had risen to only 8.2 percent at the end of 2006, from 3.8 percent at the end of 1998, the year when emerging stock markets reached their low point after the emerging market sell-off that began in 1997.

People who invest through 401(k) plans appear to be taking even less risk in emerging markets and foreign developed markets. These investors had just 5.4 percent of their money in international stock funds and only 0.7 percent in emerging market funds at the end of 2005, the most recent data for these plans, according to Hewitt Associates.[13]

Many investors may also have overall portfolio allocations that are still tilted too much toward safety, with large allocations to Treasury bills, notes, and bonds and other fixed-income securities.

For example, if you view mutual fund holdings as a sort of overall portfolio, investors had 55.5 percent of their assets in stocks and 44.5 percent in bonds and money-market funds at the end of 2006, according to AMG Data Services. That is still a pretty cautious blend of risk and will not produce the returns investors will want in the future.

Younger investors, who have many years before retirement and, therefore, the ability to absorb the ups and downs that come with more risk, should have a much higher percentage of stocks in their portfolios.

T. Rowe Price, the mutual fund company, recommends that 25-year-old investors who are saving for retirement in 2047 should have 90 percent of their portfolios in stocks and just 10 percent in fixed-income securities. Investors planning to retire as soon as 10 years from now should have a portfolio that is 70 percent stocks. These recommendations are based on analysis that assumes investors may live 30 years past retirement.

Another reason it is hard to get a specific feel for risk appetite is that investors do not understand the long-term risk they need to take and often are too focused on the short-term risk they are taking.

"Investors will express a risk tolerance that really reflects their short-term view and use this view to make investing decisions, when they really are long-term investors," said Jerome Clark, an asset allocation portfolio manager at T. Rowe Price. This problem can leave many investors short of the appropriate risk and potential capital appreciation they need for a long-term financial plan.

Other investors can believe that they are not taking a lot of risk while in fact their portfolios could be off the charts.

This is true because investors can be easily fooled if they decide to run with the crowd. If you tell investors that stocks are going to keep rising and that if they wait to jump on they will miss the gravy train, they are easily blinded to the risk they are taking.

That was the case in the late 1990s when risk was turned on its head and became the threat of missing big, easy profits. Millions of Americans threw their savings—and money borrowed against their homes' equity or on their credit cards—at stocks, especially technology and telecommunications stocks, many of which had no earnings then and never produced any subsequently.

This was not surprising, since financial bubbles tend to sweep up all and sundry into their madness. Stocks had five straight great years by the end of the 1990s, and stock market analysts touted the stocks of all kinds of companies—even if they were selling out of these stocks themselves.

The holding of company stock in 401(k) plans is a prime example of the mismatch between the perception of risk and its reality. At the end of 2005, the 401(k) plans of investors who owned company stock had 36.8 percent of their money in company stocks, according to Hewitt Associates.[14]

Well before the collapse of Enron and WorldCom, it was clear that holding too much of any one stock was very risky. And although the failures of these big companies and the bursting of the stock market bubble have reduced the holdings of company stock in 401(k) plans significantly, 36.8 percent of a portfolio is still way too much.

But as Hewitt Associates notes in the commentary in its report on the holdings in 401(k) plans, investors tend to believe that company stock is less risky than other domestic or foreign equities.[15]

Despite these risk shortfalls, let's not be unfair to the appetite and learning curve of American investors. Their risk exposure has been expanding for years, except for what appears to be a small retreat after the stock market crash. So this means they are going in the right direction and can adapt to taking on more risk.

In part because their risk tolerance had been so low, Americans were taking on more risk all during the bull market for stocks from 1982 to 2000. This shift occurred as a new generation came of age and grew to trust stocks the way their parents, children of the Depression, learned to distrust them.

The household balance sheet of Americans as a group shows that stocks as a percentage of financial assets went from 20.5 percent in 1980 to the 1999 high of 50 percent, before the recent decline, according to data from the Federal Reserve.

The mix of assets held in mutual funds shows a similar shift, with stocks as a percentage of total mutual fund assets rising as high as 57.9 percent in 2000, from 24.6 percent in 1992, when AMG Data Services began collecting these mutual fund numbers. As noted earlier, this share is now a little lower.

Risk has been increased in American portfolios not only by adding more American stocks but also by beginning to add stocks from abroad, especially as the fall in the dollar in the past several years has made buying abroad much more profitable.

Treasury data on the purchase of foreign stocks by Americans shows that the dollar total has risen dramatically. Annual net purchases of foreign stocks did not get over $10 billion until 1989 and by 2005 they had zoomed to over $127 billion. For the 12 months through November of 2006, Americans were buying foreign stocks at a pace that would bring them close to the 2005 total. Purchases of foreign bonds, which used to be more popular than foreign stocks, totaled $47.1 billion in 2005, the third highest yearly total ever in the history of the Treasury data. At the furious pace of buying through November of 2006, Americans were en route to more than double that 2005 total and set a new annual record.

To finish this chapter, we offer a bit of advice about the long term, risk, and the fear of risk, from Robert J. Barbera, chief economist at Investment Technology Group (ITG), a New York brokerage and technology firm. "Remember this when you think that emerging stock and bond markets look too risky or that small-cap stocks look too risky," he says. "They all looked risky in 1990 and look at where they are now."

2

More Than Stocks, More Than Bonds

There was a time when once you had learned about diversifying your portfolio, the rest was pretty easy. Never hold too much of any one stock or any one sector of stocks, and buy abroad, as well as at home.

The rest of the world's stock markets, and other asset classes like bonds and commodities, provided what investors needed to diversify—foreign markets and other investments than stocks that would move in the opposite direction of equities in the United States.

The idea of diversification is one of the best thoughts to come out of investment thinking in the past century. Harry Markowitz won the Nobel Memorial Prize in Economic Science in 1990 for showing that buying a variety of stocks, even risky stocks, would reduce the overall level of risk in a portfolio below that of the individual stocks themselves. It did not take long to apply this modern portfolio theory (MPT) to investing abroad.

Diversification is still a central argument for buying foreign stocks today.

But that route to diversification is no longer so easy. The world's stock markets are becoming more and more in tune with each other and following each other's lead.

This diminished benefit of diversification in stocks abroad is another consequence of the globalization of the world's economies and the around-the-world fight against inflation. The growth of companies with a global reach has also contributed to this synchronization of markets, as has the speed of communication, which allows more and more people to know what is going on every second in markets around the world.

Problems with diversification into foreign stocks, of course, spell trouble for all investors, big or small, if it does not reduce the risk of loss in your portfolio. For the authors of this book, troubles with diversification are even a bigger issue: We are urging investors to buy more stocks abroad at a time when these purchases may not make their overall portfolios more diversified. So we cannot argue that it is easy to contain the added risk you are taking on by buying more foreign stocks to increase your potential returns.

In addition, one of the most promising new diversifying alternatives—diversification by sectors—is not proving to be as effective as once hoped.

What we want to do in this chapter is explain what is happening with diversification and show that there are ways around the snares being created by the follow-the-leader nature of the world's stock markets. And while we say the benefits of diversification abroad and by sector have been diminished, we are not saying they have disappeared. So these strategies will still help—just not as much.

But we also have to say that in many cases you will just have to grin and bear it. The need to add risk to increase potential returns and the opportunities offered by investing abroad overwhelm concerns about the diminished benefits from diversification.

DIVERSIFYING ABROAD

Diversification is, on the surface, a simple concept and we are not going to spend a lot of time explaining it or why it is a good idea, because we think that is a given.

The idea is that your portfolio needs to have something that is going up when other parts of the portfolio are going down. Knowing that something in your portfolio is likely to go up no matter what will make it easier for you to sleep. And diversification can protect your portfolio from absolute routs.

In statistical terms, you are looking for a lack of correlation in picking the investments in your portfolio. Among your stocks, you look for equity groups or sectors that tend to move in different directions—for example, by buying both the blue chips in the Standard & Poor's 500 stock index and the often unheard-of smaller-cap stocks that are in the Russell 2000 Index.

In 2001, when the total return for the S&P 500 dropped 11.9 percent, the total return for the Russell 2000 rose 2.5 percent; in 1998, when the total return for the S&P 500 was a gain of 28.6 percent, the return for the Russell 2000 dropped 2.6 percent.[1] So when one was up the other was down. That is diversification. To reduce risk you have to accept the fact that something in your portfolio may not always be doing well.

In 2000, both indexes had a decline in total return, with the S&P 500 down 9.1 percent while the Russell 2000 was off just 3 percent. They did not move in opposite directions, but that is often what a low correlation actually is: not a rise versus a fall, but a much smaller rise or a much smaller decline. These different paces in the same direction change the risk of your portfolio. That is, it is better to have half your portfolio falling 3 percent while the rest is dropping 9.1 percent, which translates into a decline in return of 6.1 percent, instead of all of it plunging 9.1 percent. You might retort that if all the portfolio were in the Russell 2000, it would have fallen just 3 percent. But that is known only with hindsight. With diversification, you have to commit yourself in advance to the fact that a variety of securities in your portfolio will move in different directions or at different paces. The simple 50–50 split of this example is diversification, but you can do a lot more.

The result of diversification is not always a smaller loss. It can be a smaller gain. In 2003, the year the stock market began its recovery from the 2000 crash, the S&P 500 had a total return of 28.7 percent while the return for the Russell 2000 was a stunning 47.3 percent. The combined return was 38 percent.

Adding Treasury bills, notes, and bonds and other fixed-income securities—a completely different asset class—gives you an even better chance of having one part of the portfolio going up while another part is falling or just creeping higher.

When the S&P 500's total return fell 11.9 percent in 2001, the return from the Lehman Brothers U.S. Aggregate Index, including Treasury securities, investment-grade corporate bonds, and mortgages, was 8.4 percent.

(The reason for the big return was that interest rates dropped sharply as the Federal Reserve cut the overnight lending rate between banks—its target federal funds rate—to 1.75 percent from 6.5 percent. Those rate cuts brought down interest rates across the board, raising bill, note, and bond prices, which move in the opposite direction of bond yields. And those price increases gave investors big capital gains, which when added to the interest paid on the bills, notes, and bonds combined for the nice return.)

In 1994, the bond market had its worst year ever since the inception of the Lehman Aggregate bond index in 1976, with an actual loss of 2.9 percent for the Lehman Aggregate and 3.4 percent for Treasury notes and bonds. But the S&P 500 stock index actually had a positive total return, including dividends, of 1.3 percent. It was a year that was miserable for bonds but flat for stocks, as the Federal Reserve drove its short-term interest rate sharply higher, to 6 percent from 3 percent, in just 12 months.

(Bonds and notes pay a set interest rate, so when the annual total return is a loss that is a really bad year, because declines in the prices of the bonds and notes are needed to turn the interest paid into a loss. In 1994, the interest paid was swamped by a decline in bond and note prices of 9.5 percent in the Treasury and other fixed-income markets, also the worst since 1976.)

This lack of correlation had also been true when looking at the performance of American stocks versus those abroad. In 1978, for example, stocks on Wall Street eked out a barely positive 0.4 percent gain for the year, based on MSCI's index for the United States. The index for the United Kingdom had a gain of 8.6 percent, in dollar terms. But that was nothing compared to the 50.1 percent gain for the Japanese index and the 63.1 percent gain for the stock index in France. In 1977, the U.S. market was off 12.2 percent, while Japan was up 13.2 percent, Germany was up 21 percent, and the United Kingdom was up 50.2 percent, all in dollar terms.

In 1992, the relationship was in the other direction, with the U.S. stock market up 4.2 percent while in the United Kingdom equities fell 7.2 percent. In Germany the market was down 11.8 percent, and in Japan stocks plunged 22.1 percent.

But this lack of correlation has disappeared in recent years, and not only in developed markets abroad but also in emerging markets.

In May and June of 2006, there was a slump in global stock markets, triggered by a sudden spike of inflation jitters in the United States. The U.S. stock market dropped 8 percent, developed markets outside the United States fell 14.9 percent, and emerging markets plunged 24.5 percent, based on MSCI data.

A study by economists at the International Monetary Fund highlights the diminishing benefits of diversifying abroad very bluntly. The study shows that although American investors are the least diversified of the investors in the four-country study (United States, Germany, United Kingdom, and Japan), they have only a "limited amount" to gain by diversifying more.[2]

Hung Tran, the deputy director of the Monetary and Capital Markets Department at the International Monetary Fund, acknowledged that this study was limited because it did not include more countries, especially emerging markets. But he said it still made a point about the rising correlations of markets around the world.

"The more that people invest overseas, the more common ownership there is, the more there will be common responses to events that move markets," he said, referring to the 2006 summer slump of global markets. "That is a fact of life and this correlation is going to increase as globalization increases."

It just takes a zero and a one to explain that correlations of stock markets around the world are rising.

A one (1) means a strong correlation in the same direction, while a minus one (–1) means a strong correlation in the opposite direction. A zero (0) means no correlation. In the analysis here we are being conservative, using five-year, or 60-month, rolling correlations. This means that each monthly correlation reading includes five years of returns from the United States compared to five years of monthly returns of a foreign market or markets. This smooths out a lot of the noise.

While the average correlation over time between the moves of U.S. stocks and those in countries abroad is still relatively low, its current level is well above that average and has held pretty constant in recent years. That is what is worrisome, because it does not seem that the rise in correlations is an aberration.

For stocks trading in so-called developed markets abroad, the average correlation has been 0.562 since December 1974, the beginning of the first five-year period of rolling monthly correlations using return data from MSCI for the United States and stock markets abroad. In the period through December 2006, the lowest correlation was 0.261 in April 1997. The highest correlation was 0.869 in April 2005.

The graph of these correlations, as seen in Figure 2.1, shows how dramatically the relationship has changed. Until August 1998, the correlation between the U.S. markets and developed stock markets abroad—from the United Kingdom and Germany to Japan and Australia—had been over 0.6 only two times in more than 23 years, in February and March of 1978. Since August 1998, the correlation has not been below 0.6 even once.

Put another way, the average correlation of the movement of U.S. stocks to stocks in developed countries abroad through July

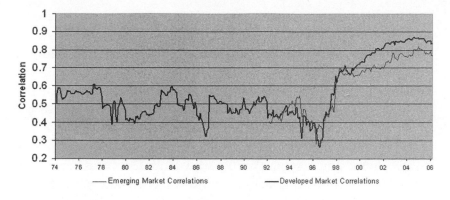

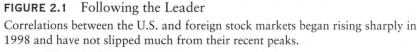

FIGURE 2.1   Following the Leader

Correlations between the U.S. and foreign stock markets began rising sharply in 1998 and have not slipped much from their recent peaks.

Source: PIMCO. Data from MSCI.

1998 was 0.482. Since then the average has been 0.790. That is a 64 percent increase in the average correlation.

Ten developed stock markets, including Germany, Italy, France, and Switzerland, registered their highest correlation levels with the American stock market in 2006. And four others, Australia, Denmark, Norway, and Sweden, reached their highest correlation levels ever in the last eight months of 2005.

This rise in correlations may not be so surprising because the stock markets in all these developed countries have become more and more alike, as have their economic policies. But there also has been a striking increase in the correlation of the movements in emerging markets to those in the United States. And that big shift up in correlations with emerging markets came at the same time as in developed markets: in the summer of 1998.

That was the year after emerging markets plunged when Thailand's sudden devaluation of its currency, the baht, triggered the worst sell-off ever in these markets. In the summer and fall of 1998 things got worse as Russia defaulted on some of its debt and devalued its own currency, the ruble. And the American stock and bond markets were roiled by the near-failure of the giant hedge fund, Long-Term Capital Management.

Clearly in the aftermath of these big market events there was a broader coming together of economic policy around the world, including in emerging markets. And it seems that this growing similarity in the goals of economic policy and the opening of markets to freer trade—that is, the general globalization of the world's economy—is making stock markets around the world move more in sync.

As in developed markets, the correlation of emerging markets to the United States went over 0.6 in August 1998 and has stayed above 0.6 since. Before then, the closest a correlation had gotten to 0.6 was 0.548 in July 1995, according to the analysis of stock market return data from MSCI that begins its monthly readings of five-year rolling correlations in December 1992.

The average correlation in all of the emerging markets covered by MSCI to the U.S. market was 0.438 from December 1992 through July 1998. Since then the average has jumped 66 percent to 0.725, almost the exact same increase in correlations, in percentage terms, seen in developed stock markets. Since May of 2005, 14 emerging stock markets, including the largest, South Korea, have registered their highest correlation levels ever compared to the United States.

In the case of both developed and emerging markets, some of the change is explained by big moves in dominant countries in each category.

Take South Korea, for example, whose stock market capitalization accounted for 15.5 percent of the MSCI emerging market index. South Korea's correlation with the American market has surged, doubling in the three years from April of 2000 to April of 2003 to 0.607. By December of 2006, the correlation level was up to 0.649.

At the same time, the correlation level was also rising sharply in the fifth largest emerging stock market, Brazil, which was 10.5 percent of the emerging market index at the end of 2006. Its correlation had jumped to 0.705 by May of 2005, more than doubling from the level in July 1998. While Brazil's correlation slipped below the 0.7 level by the end of 2006, it is still one of the reasons that the overall correlation level of emerging markets has been over 0.7 since September of 2002.

These higher levels of correlation mean that reducing the overall risk in your portfolio is more difficult. And that is just when stock markets are in their normal up and down cycles. Making this rise in correlations more of a problem is the fact that when there is a big sell-off in markets, especially one led by the United States, stock markets around the world are even more inclined to move in the same direction, which, unfortunately, is down.

Research by Kirt C. Butler, associate professor of finance at Michigan State University, and Domingo Castelo Joaquin, associate professor of finance at the College of Business at Illinois State University, shows that correlations pick up in big sell-offs.

"The fundamental rationale for international portfolio diversification is that it expands the opportunities for gains from portfolio diversification beyond those that are available through domestic securities," the two wrote in their paper on this issue. "However, if international stock market correlations are higher than normal in bear markets, then international portfolio diversification will fail to yield the promised gains just when they are needed most."[3]

Because of these higher than normal correlations in big market sell-offs, the authors estimate that in the worst of bear markets the annual return to investors could be about two percentage points lower than expected in a portfolio equally split between domestic and foreign stocks.

What should investors do when confronted with the rising trend in correlations of world stock markets and the fact that these stock markets are even more closely correlated when stocks are falling?

Butler and Joaquin said that if this high bear market correlation continues, investors will have to try to anticipate and avoid markets that will have higher correlations with the U.S. stock market in future downturns. In a bit of economic analysis understatement, they concluded that such forecasting will be difficult. "Because of the infrequency and randomness of extreme market events, this prediction is difficult to make with precision," they wrote.[4]

The authors themselves chose two different responses. Joaquin cut the global portion of his portfolio, which included both U.S. and foreign stocks, to 20 percent from 40 percent. "Foreign equities are not as reliable a cushion during market downturns as I originally assumed [before the study]," Joaquin said in an interview by e-mail. "And I can still take advantage of profit opportunities in foreign markets indirectly by investing in U.S. firms with substantial operations in other countries."

Butler left his portfolio alone. He is still betting on the higher returns he can expect from abroad over time, because of the higher risk. And so the reduced benefits from diversification mean less to him.

"My thinking was and is that international investing is still the only game that's in town," he said in an interview by e-mail. "I am a buy-and-hold investor that looks toward my long-term risk/return exposure. I generally do not try to time the market."

Some investors may choose to ignore the rise in correlations because there are analysts who argue that they will not remain this high. Professor Geert Bekaert, the Leon G. Cooperman Professor of Finance and Economics at Columbia Business School, is in this camp. "There are good reasons to suspect some higher correlations through the process of integration (both economic and financial) and that should also increase correlations between emerging and developed markets," he said in an e-mail, when commenting on the sharp rise in correlations between stocks in the United States and stocks in emerging markets. But he added that "the correlations you report for emerging markets will, in my opinion, turn out to be lousy predictors of future correlations—they will be lower."

We are not in agreement. But this does mean that there is not an open-and-shut case against the benefits of diversifying to foreign stock markets in the years ahead. And this is why investors have to continue to pay attention to the changing financial environment.

And now a little surprise and another reason to keep your eye on what is going on: The surprise is that the correlation between the S&P 500 and the Russell 2000 stock indexes has been high recently, which could make the Russell 2000 less dependable for diversification. At the end of 2006, the correlation with the S&P 500 was up to 0.819. While it was heading down a bit at the end of the year—and was below its high of 0.903 in November of 1991—the correlation was up from a low of 0.583 in March of 2000. In 2005, when the Russell 2000 and the S&P 500 had almost the same performance, gains of 4.6 percent and 4.9 percent, respectively, their average correlation was 0.814. When the correlation averaged 0.651 in 2001, the Russell rose 2.5 percent while the S&P 500 dropped 11.9 percent.

DIVERSIFYING BY ASSET CLASS

While diversification abroad, as a way to reduce risk in a stock portfolio, has become less rewarding because of rising correlations, diversification by asset class is still holding its own. Correlations between stocks and commodities and stocks and bonds are still very low, although there will always be periods when they all follow each other.

This is not only a good idea because of the theory of diversification; it is also a good idea in a world where financial advice—including this book—is ever more available to the everyday investor. There are many more voices out there advising investors to do this or that. A lot of this advice is to jump onto this bandwagon or to jump off of that bandwagon. And because it is so much easier for retail investors to put this advice into action, diversification is a good hedge against the problem with following a lot of different financial advice: Some of it is wrong.

Look at the fixed-income market after the stock market crash. In 2001, the bond market easily outperformed the stock market, despite several wrenching ups and downs in interest rates. In 2002, many fixed-income analysts and financial writers were worried about rising interest rates, which would mean a bad year for the bond market. It didn't happen. Longer-term interest rates actually fell sharply in 2002, producing a 10.3 percent return in the broad bond market, and more in the Treasury sector, according to the Lehman Aggregate bond index. And even though short-term interest rates did go up in 2004, longer-term yields actually slipped slightly, and the bond market, including Treasuries, corporate bonds, and mortgage-backed securities, turned in a return of 4.3 percent for the year. A diversified portfolio including bonds would have rewarded investors for these unexpected performances.

One way to view the benefits of diversification into other assets than stocks is to look at the returns for a portfolio of stocks,

---

Some longtime investors who think a lot about risk, like Peter Bernstein, the author of *Against the Gods: The Remarkable Story of Risk* (John Wiley & Sons, 1996), want to have an added hedge in their portfolio just in case the worst happens. A hedge is a bet against your main strategy—which is why you pray you are wrong to make this bet. You should hedge against a low-probability occurrence that could have very big consequences.

Here is an example: If you love stocks, load up, but put a small portion of your portfolio into long-dated zero coupon bonds—5 percent to 10 percent, say, depending on the seriousness of the consequences if the worst happens. You pay well under the face value for these bonds because there are no cash interest payments to you. You get the implied interest payments back when the bond matures and you are paid its face value. If something bad happens that drives interest rates and stocks sharply lower, like a recession, 30-year zero coupon bonds do very well. If interest rates fall by two full percentage points, the value of the zero coupon bonds would go up 60 percent.

bonds, commodities, and cash over time—for example, over the past 10 years. The surprise here is not that an all-stock portfolio did better over the long run. The surprise is that the diversified portfolio did not do badly at all, in comparison. And it proved to be less volatile. So there may have been a few more restful nights for the investors who were diversified, although it is quite true that they would have had fewer parties in the late 1990s.

For this demonstration (see Table 2.1) we used a portfolio of 55 percent stocks (from the S&P 500); 30 percent bonds (using the Lehman Aggregate bond index); 10 percent commodities (using the Goldman Sachs Commodity Index or GSCI Total Return, which includes crude oil, natural gas, copper, gold, wheat, coffee, live cattle, and lean hogs among its commodities); and 5 percent cash (using a 30-day Treasury bill).

Remember that this portfolio, for the simplicity of comparing asset allocation alternatives, has all its equity money in the S&P 500 and all of its fixed-income money in investment-grade bonds. A real portfolio should have that equity money apportioned among

TABLE 2.1 Diversify Your Worries: Try Bonds and Commodities

	S&P 500 Stock Index	30-Day Treasury Bill	Lehman Aggregate Bond Index	Goldman Sachs Commodity Index	55% Stock/ 30% Bond/ 10% Commodity/ 5% Cash
3 Years through 2006	10.4%	3.0%	3.7%	7.7%	8.1%
5 Years through 2006	6.2%	2.3%	5.1%	14.8%	7.0%
10 Years through 2006	8.4%	3.6%	6.2%	4.7%	7.7%
15 Years through 2006	10.6%	3.8%	6.5%	6.2%	9.0%
20 Years through 2006	11.8%	4.5%	7.4%	9.8%	10.4%
25 Years through 2006	13.4%	5.3%	9.5%	9.5%	11.9%
30 Years through 2006	12.5%	6.0%	8.4%	9.7%	11.1%

Returns from a diversified portfolio, compared to the returns of its components, over seven time periods.
Source: Ibbotson Associates.
Data from the Federal Reserve, Goldman Sachs, Lehman Brothers, and Standard & Poor's.

the S&P 500, small-cap stocks, foreign developed markets, and foreign emerging markets. And some of the bond money could be in high-yield junk bonds or abroad. More on this in Chapter 8.

As we said, an all-stock portfolio rules the roost, except for the five-year period ending in 2006, according to calculations by Ibbotson Associates. But as the time periods lengthen, the overall 55/30/10/5 portfolio does better, compared to the other components. In fact, it just about outduels all but stocks.

As can be seen in Table 2.1, in the three-year run the best performer was the S&P 500 stock index, with a compound annual return of 10.4 percent. The 55/30/10/5 portfolio was second at 8.1 percent, followed by the commodity index at 7.7 percent. The Lehman Aggregate bond index had a compound annual return of 3.7 percent, and the 30-day Treasury bill came in at 3 percent.

In the five-year run, the commodity index won, with a compound annual return of 14.8 percent, followed by the 7 percent compound annual return for the 55/30/10/5 portfolio. Stocks were third with a total return, including dividends, of 6.2 percent and the Lehman Aggregate bond index was fourth with a return of 5.1 percent. The 30-day Treasury bill came in at 2.3 percent.

Over 15 years, the compound annual return for the overall portfolio was 9 percent, compared to 10.6 percent for stocks. Over 20 years, the portfolio's compound annual return was 10.4 percent, compared to 11.8 percent for stocks. Over 30 years, the portfolio's compound annual return was 11.1 percent, compared to 12.5 percent for stocks.

Now, let us be clear. You are paying for this diversification. Over time, the difference between a compound annual return of 12.5 percent, with an all-stock portfolio, and 11.1 percent, with the portfolio of diversified assets, is significant. A $10,000 portfolio of just the S&P 500, without any more additions, grew to $342,433 after 30 years, based on historical returns, while the diversified portfolio increased to only $235,192.

But the risk level of the two portfolios is also significantly different. The standard deviation of the all-stock portfolio, based on

performance from 1977, is 15.6, compared to 9.6 for the diversified portfolio. So what do you do?

There is something to help you make these choices. It is called
the Sharpe ratio. It effectively equalizes the risk between the two
investments and then tells you which is giving you the better return for the risk taken (the higher ratio).[5]

The 55/30/10/5 portfolio has a Sharpe ratio of 1.2. The all-
stock portfolio has a Sharpe ratio of 0.87 percent. So, for the
equalized risk, the diversified portfolio is more attractive.

If you want a higher return, you have to take on more risk.
This is easy to do by adding more stocks and reducing the portions of the other assets in the portfolio.

The first portion to go is the 5 percent cash. If that had been
shifted into stocks, raising the allocation to 60 percent of the portfolio, the compound annual return for the portfolio would have
moved to 11.5 percent over 30 years, while the risk level would
have risen to 10.3. The Sharpe ratio would be 1.16, only slightly
lower than that of the 55/30/10/5 portfolio with a little more return.

You can go much further. Some mutual fund companies suggest that investors planning to retire in forty years should have 90
percent or more of their portfolios in stocks and the rest in bonds.
With that asset allocation in effect over the 30 years ending in
2006, the portfolio return was 12.2 percent, compared to 12.5
percent for all stocks and 11.1 percent for the original portfolio
with 55 percent in stocks.

The risk level of the 90/10 portfolio moved up to 14.2, compared to 15.6 for all stocks. The Sharpe ratio of the 90/10 portfolio is 0.92. That makes it a bit more attractive for the risk involved
than the all-stock portfolio, and over 30 years the 90/10 portfolio
grows to $316,072, just slightly less than the all-stock portfolio.

And because the return of the 90/10 portfolio is significantly
higher than the returns on the 55/30/10/5 portfolio and the 60/40
portfolio, the difference in the Sharpe ratios should be ignored.

In going for higher risk and higher returns, first concentrate on
building a portfolio with a higher return and then use the Sharpe
ratio to help you choose among alternatives of similar returns.

If this all sounds a little contradictory after reading the first chapter, it is, a little. But that is not unusual in investing. We still want investors to take on more risk. But because investors have different tolerances, they will take on different levels of risk. So diversification by assets is a way to take on more risk and worry a little bit less.

There are so many ups and downs in the market that it is worth paying for some hedging against bad years, as was the case for stocks in the six years through 2005. This is a choice each investor has to make, depending on your tolerance and when in your life you are making the decision. Asset allocation into bonds looks much better near retirement than it does at age 25.

And if your diversified portfolio winds up having more risk than you started out with—but less than an all-stock portfolio—then there is nothing to worry about. You have increased your risk. And, anyway, we are not arguing for all-stock portfolios all the time. We are just showing you the trade-offs.

Now let us just show you how bad—which is good, from a diversification point of view—the correlations are between stocks and bonds and stocks and commodities. Bonds and commodities have a mind of their own, as you can see from a quick glance at Figure 2.2.

Using the S&P 500 for the stock market and the Lehman Aggregate index for bonds, the average correlation is 0.251 from 1980 through 2006, using five-year, or 60-month, rolling correlations. The high correlation was 0.599 in September 1997, and the low correlation was minus 0.37 in March 2006. As of the end of 2006, the correlation was minus 0.283. Remember, a minus 1 means a strong correlation in the opposite direction. As for Treasury Inflation Protected Securities (TIPS), the correlation is also negative, but based on a very short history, since these now-popular securities were first issued in 1997. The average correlation to stocks is minus 0.253. At the end of 2006, the correlation was minus 0.298.

The correlation between stocks and commodities, using the 24 commodities in the GSCI Total Return index, is also pretty negative. The correlation has averaged minus 0.027 since 1986. The high correlation was 0.303 in December 1996, while the low

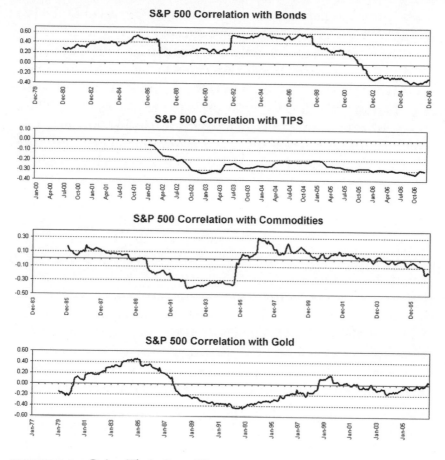

FIGURE 2.2 Going Their Own Way

Correlations between U.S. stocks and other asset classes show that they are good diversification additions to your portfolio.

Source: PIMCO. Data from Goldman Sachs, Lehman Brothers, Chicago Mercantile Exchange, and Standard & Poor's.

correlation was minus 0.413 in November 1992. As of the end of 2006, the correlation was minus 0.176.

The correlation between stocks and gold is negative, but slightly less negative than between stocks and the broad commodity index. Gold had been a classic portfolio diversifier in the past but fell from grace after its price plunged in the late 1990s. But now that the price of an ounce has breached $600 again, gold could come back. The average correlation is minus 0.051. The high was 0.462 in December 1984; the low was minus 0.446 in October 1982. At the end of 2006, the correlation was 0.045.

SECTORS

Another way to reduce risk in a portfolio is to invest in stocks globally by sectors, rather than by country.

At the end of the 1990s investment firms and mutual funds realigned their strategies to concentrate more on sectors, and many funds and indexes have popped up to give investors the opportunity to take advantage of this approach to diversification. But as we noted at the beginning of this chapter, sector investing does not seem to be as beneficial as a diversifier as first hoped.

The concept grows logically out of the changes in markets brought on by globalization. As more and more companies have a global reach, including a significant portion of sales abroad, the less their home country's economy may impact on earnings and growth. In fact, this argument is now used by many, including Professor Joaquin, who was quoted earlier, who argued that American investors can get the benefit of investing abroad by just buying the big global companies like General Electric and Coca-Cola that are based in the United States. As of the end of 2006, the companies in the S&P 500 had, all together, about 45 percent of their sales outside the United States, according to Standard & Poor's.

Another argument for sector investing is that if you just diversify by country using main market indexes, you can get big distortions in your portfolio.

Take the example of ownership of indexes in the United States, Germany, and Japan as a way to diversify a portfolio. While the foreign portion of this portfolio may be diversified by country, sector proponents argue that it is not well diversified by sector. They point out that in the American portion of the portfolio the automotive sector accounts for just 0.5 percent, while in Germany autos are 11.4 percent of the weighting of the stock market, and that rises to 12.2 percent in Japan, according to MSCI indexes at the end of 2006. A more extreme example is Finland, where the local stock market is dominated by the technology sector in the name of Nokia, which makes up 45.6 percent of the Finnish MSCI index; so investors have really bought a sector rather than a country.

And with the whole world to choose from, sector proponents contend that American investors should not be deciding if they want General Motors or Citibank in their portfolios. A more logical choice is between General Motors and Toyota, the kind of choice that will keep investors focused on finding the best company, whether it is based at home or abroad.[6]

Stefano Cavaglia, managing director at UBS O'Connor LLC, has been a longtime advocate of the sector or industry approach. "The profession was so fossilized by the country approach," he said, explaining one of the reasons for his delving into the sector alternative, which began when he was teaching at the City University Business School in London.

But he acknowledges that sector investing is not the be-all and end-all, especially now that data shows that its benefits, in terms of returns and diversification, have been on the decline since 2001. But, he said, "the point is that you cannot ignore the sector effects anymore." So, he concludes, the two approaches should be used together.

And since we are advocating portfolios with bigger shares of foreign stocks in them, using a sector filter is another good way to approach the stock selection process, even if it is not as good a diversifier as it was.

3

What Can Go Wrong

This chapter is about the investing environment and what could happen to it in the years ahead.

To examine that question we look at several threats—deficits, market bubbles, and recessions—and at one country—China. In this chapter we assess the seriousness of these threats. Later in the book, we suggest some portfolio adjustments that can be made to deal with the changing financial environment.

Of course, other things can go wrong, including terrorism. But these are the kinds of events one cannot include in a forecast, although it is pretty certain that there will be more terrorist attacks. There are also likely to be disruptions in the supply of oil and other events that will be more unexpected and surprising. We will just leave them in the exogenous category.

Of deficits, there are two, the current account deficit and the federal budget deficit. We think the current account deficit, which is the gap in the trade of goods and services that the United States has with the rest of the world, is not a big threat, although many analysts would disagree with us. The federal budget deficit has not had a noticeable impact on interest rates so far, but it could be surprisingly disruptive in the future.

Market bubbles will be unavoidable in the future. In fact, the breeding ground for them is more fertile than in the past. But recessions—which could be caused by a bursting bubble—are more worrisome. Recessions will confront the Federal Reserve with its biggest challenge: avoiding the misstep that could bring on a debilitating round of deflation.

Then there is China, which figures in the current account story, in the future level of interest rates, and in the future pace of inflation in the United States. China has already helped keep both interest rates and inflation here lower than they would have been and, at the same time, helped cover our record current account deficit. The question is how long all these benefits will continue to accrue to American investors and consumers.

WHAT CAN GO WRONG: CURRENT ACCOUNT DEFICIT

The current account has been a worry for the government, economists, and investors for decades. It was most recently on the front burner in the 1980s. Back then the Cassandra call of many excited analysts was to beware of the twin deficits, as the current account deficit shot up to $161 billion in 1987 from a surplus of $5 billion in 1981, and the federal budget deficit jumped to $221 billion in 1986 from $79 billion in 1981.

That threat passed. But the argument that the current account deficit is unsustainable in the long run is irrefutable, and it is the argument that has many analysts worried today. The current account deficit, they note, is now over $800 billion, a record and five times the size it was in the 1980s, as can be seen in Figure 3.1. Americans continue to spend beyond their means, consuming more than they produce at home and importing the difference from abroad, with foreigners financing that difference. But there is a limit—in the long run—to foreigners' willingness to continue

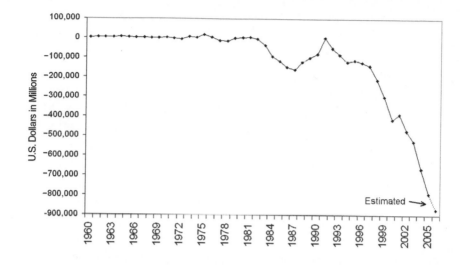

FIGURE 3.1 Can It Continue?

The U.S. current account deficit, which is the gap in the trade of goods and services between the United States and the rest of the world, has grown dramatically.

Source: Bureau of Economic Analysis.

this kind of lending to finance our current account deficit, they say.

That day of reckoning, when it comes, will shake up the U.S. economy in all the wrong ways, with a falling dollar, rising interest rates, and rising inflation. The biggest worry is that the current account deficit could create a crisis, where all of these things happen quickly. For investors, that would be a nightmare, with stocks, bonds, and the dollar all down sharply at the same time, the economy in a slump, and no place for investors to hide.

So the United States, as this argument goes, is dependent upon the kindness of strangers, who might not always be kind. And, therefore, Americans should get their collective financial house in order and shrink the current account deficit. This means cuts in government spending, higher taxes, and a tighter monetary policy that would reduce private sector borrowing by raising interest rates.

That argument is right in the long term. But the long term is the wrong view to take of the current account problem. We are all dead in the long run, as John Maynard Keynes said, so sustainability is not the right issue. The real argument about the current account deficit from an investor's point of view is how long the unsustainable can be sustained. Or to return to Keynes, what happens before we die? The answer is that we live, or in the case of the current account, that it is sustainable in the medium term.

But while that means the worst can be put off for a while—maybe long enough to get the current account deficit under control—the current account deficit will still have its fallout, and that is not going to be pleasant. Inflation and interest rates will be higher than otherwise would be the case and there is a chance of an error. The then troublesome current account deficit was a player in the background of the squabbling among the United States and other nations that was followed by the 1987 stock market crash.

There are several reasons, however, why a current account crisis is not around the corner and why this deficit can be sustained in the medium term.

One is that it is in the interest of emerging market countries, like China, to continue to provide the financing needed to bridge the deficit gap. This is because much of the American spending that creates the deficit is on products from emerging market countries. And that buying is fueling these countries' economic growth and creating millions of new jobs.

Another reason is that it is in the interest of emerging market countries to keep their currencies relatively stable compared to the dollar, because that means their exports to the United States remain competitively priced. If these emerging market currencies rise sharply in value, the exports sold in the United States will become more expensive, cutting into sales abroad and economic growth back home.

In addition, low inflation around the world creates an environment in which foreign central banks are more likely to prevent a sharp rise in the value of their currencies against the dollar—to avoid domestic deflationary pressures—and are thus more likely to help fund our current account deficit if private investors get weary. Both goals are achieved by buying dollars and then reinvesting those dollars in the United States, mostly in Treasury securities and other bonds.

Such foreign central bank dollar buying cannot be sustained indefinitely, because it would lead to excessively loose monetary policies in the foreigners' countries, generating inflation and/or stock and other asset price bubbles. But low inflation makes this central bank buying sustainable longer.

In fact, the dominant risk scenario in the global economy right now is deflation (too many goods chasing too few buyers), not corrosive inflation (too many buyers chasing too few goods). And as long as this is the dominant risk case, there is no fear of the inflationary consequences that would limit foreign central banks' appetite for dollars, if and when private investors don't want to fund our current account deficit.

So the United States is not hostage to the kindness of strangers, but rather, hostage to strangers acting in their own best interest: They are choosing to print their currencies to buy dollars so they can prevent or temper the appreciation of their currencies and more fully employ their underemployed workers. It really is that simple.

This self-interest has clearly been shown by how much some foreign central banks have entered the foreign exchange market to buy dollars, which in turn keeps their home currencies from rising in value against the American currency. Those dollars are then recycled to the United States, by purchasing Treasury securities, agency bonds, corporate bonds, and some stocks. And that flow into the United States, along with that from private investors, is the so-called loan or financing that covers or bridges the current account deficit.

This buying by central banks reached its recent peak in the 12 months ending in September 2004, with total purchases of $245 billion, according to Treasury data. At the time that was more than 28 percent of the total net foreign inflow, official and private, into U.S. bonds and stocks.

But the data also show that the foreign private sector is still more than a willing lender to finance the current account deficit. Since that peak buying of bonds and stocks by foreign central banks, their share of the total dropped down to just under 16 percent, or a $173 billion, for the 12-month period ending in November 2006. In the same period, private investors raised their share to just over 84 percent, or a total of $918 billion.

Of course, China has been a big buyer, as it has done what it has been expected to do to keep the value of its currency, the yuan, tied as closely as possible to the dollar and, in turn, promote economic growth and new jobs at home. In the two years through November 2006, China's holding of Treasury bills, notes, and bonds jumped 57 percent to $346.5 billion, leaving it second only to Japan in ownership of Treasury securities. (Japan built its commanding lead, with $637.4 billion of Treasury securities in November 2006, with an unprecedented 15-month spree of dollar buying and yen selling that ended in the first quarter of 2004. The more than 35 trillion yen spent to buy dollars was aimed at keeping the yen from rising in value against the dollar and thereby cutting into a driving force of the revival of Japan's economy, its export business. In other words, it was doing then what China is doing now, tying its currency to the dollar.) The fourth- and-fifth ranked countries on the list of top holders of Treasury bills, notes, and bonds are South Korea and Taiwan, two other big players in emerging markets.

Timothy F. Geithner, the president of the Federal Reserve Bank of New York, has pointed to this kind of foreign exchange rate arrangement as one reason cited for the sustainability of the current account deficit.

"There is also a view that the exchange rate arrangements that exist in the present context—the substantial share of the world economy that shadows the dollar—should increase our confidence that this pattern of imbalances could be financed without stress for some time," he said in January 2006.[1]

But he said that these ties to the dollar will be unwound, in part because they will eventually run counter to the domestic goals of these countries. When that happens, it will be up to the private investors from abroad to fill in the funding gap left by the central banks to cover the cost of the current account deficit—or there will be trouble.

We think that trouble can be avoided, which puts us in agreement with Alan Greenspan, the former chairman of the Federal Reserve, based on comments made during an interview at PIMCO's Tri-Annual Client Conference in March 2006—with McCulley asking the questions.

When asked how worried he was about the current account deficit, Greenspan said that "we will get out from under this" with rising interest rates and a falling dollar that will curb consumption in the United States while making our exports more attractive abroad. And that, he said, will "stop the process" and begin to shrink the current account deficit. He said he did not expect a crisis that would result in much slower growth and higher unemployment.

"I would think that means," he concluded, "it is an interesting analytical process to be watching but it is not really that all-important from an economic evaluation point of view."

Another reason investors need not worry that much is that keeping the tie to the dollar in an emerging market country is not as difficult as it might seem—aside from the protectionist pressure from the United States to untie the link.

First, a central bank cannot lose money by printing its currency in an economic sense, even though it can from an accounting perspective, if it buys something that goes down in price, measured in its own currency, which the dollar will eventually. The beauty, or bane, of a fiat currency, which is backed by the promise of a government rather than a hard asset like gold, is the power to create nominal purchasing power for nothing.

Second, currency intervention is not symmetric: Protesting an appreciating currency is very different from defending a depreciating one. The reason is that resisting a currency's rise in value is done with that country's own money—the money the central bank prints. But defending a currency has to be done with accumulated foreign currencies—a central bank's foreign currency reserves—

and/or borrowed money. In fact, defending a currency from falling has proven all but impossible over time because most central banks will quickly run out of funds and currency speculators know this, which adds a big degree of difficulty to this maneuver. But keeping a currency from rising in value can be done, as Japan proved in 2003 and 2004 and as China is still proving today.

What is needed to solve the current account problem is a big shift in the global pattern of economic growth, with the rest of the world growing faster and buying more from the United States, while the United States and its consumers slow down. Short of this, which is not a plan that is easily orchestrated, the solution is a dollar that falls so low that it has no place to go but up. That would reenergize the foreign private sector appetite for dollar-denominated assets, attracting more permanent capital flows into the United States. Such a lower level for the dollar would, of course, be negative for U.S. consumers—hiking import prices and restoring some degree of pricing power to American producers in their home market. So inflation would also move higher.

ANOTHER WORLD

The global foreign exchange regime that is today based on fiat currencies that are relatively freely traded is a world away from the 1945–1971 regime known as Bretton Woods, which was anchored by a real or hard asset: the commitment of the United States to exchange one ounce of gold for $35, while everybody else fixed their currencies to the dollar.

In the early years of Bretton Woods, the world's greatest concern was that this foreign exchange regime would beget either a chronic shortage of dollars if the United States ran a balanced current account or a global surplus of dollars relative to the U.S. stock of gold if the United States ran current account deficits.

Fears of the flaw were well-founded, as America moved from small surpluses in the 1960s to small current account deficits in the 1970s. This change created a global glut of dollars relative to Uncle Sam's stock of gold, forcing other countries—notably France, but also Japan—to buy massive amounts of dollars to maintain their pegged currencies versus the dollar. Fearing the domestic inflationary consequences, these countries, led by France, tired of doing this and asked the United States to honor its commitment to exchange gold for the dollars that they did not want. America refused and the Bretton Woods arrangement died: The United States closed the gold window for good in 1971, and two years later, after repeated attempts to make the now unworkable work, the developed world moved to a floating exchange rate regime.

But it was not a pure float. Rather, after Bretton Woods, the world adopted a managed floating regime, sometimes called a dirty float. Although many may disagree, there is nothing wrong with dirty floating exchange rates rather than putatively pure market-driven exchange rates. In a world where currency is just backed by a government promise, world markets themselves are hostage to the ways and means of sovereigns with printing presses. Money is what sovereigns say it is, unlike the case of Bretton Woods and previous gold-backed currency regimes.

Accordingly, the concept of pure market-determined exchange rates becomes an intellectual oxymoron when sovereigns own the printing presses and get their ink (rather than gold) for free. Dirty floating, as opposed to either mechanical adherence to pegged exchange rates or pure floating, represents the enlightened exercise of national sovereignty. Indeed, a measure of the maturity of a country is the freedom to determine its own monetary policy in pursuit of its own best national interest.

But such a further fall in the dollar need not become a crisis—as long as appreciating nondollar currencies are more painful to the rest of the world than a falling dollar is for the United States. As long as China and other emerging markets continue to be mercantilist (see "What Can Go Wrong: China") and want to keep their export-based economies growing, there is a reason for them to keep the dollar from falling sharply and their currencies from rising. And the mechanism to do this, selling the home currency and buying dollars, will continue to help fund the current account deficit gap.

With the world having won the war against inflation, the inflationary implications of a falling dollar are also less of a problem for the United States. A falling dollar would be a big problem for us if, and only if, we had an inflationary problem and/or the Fed thought we had an inflationary problem regardless of whether we actually did. Neither of these conditions exists right now.

So, in the long run, the unsustainable is still unsustainable. But between here and there, foreign central banks—operating in their countries' own mercantilist best interests—will happily buy dollars when foreign private sector investors do not want to fill the current account deficit gap. But right now foreign private investors are doing just that: playing the leading role in filling the gap.

The United States is not begging for foreigners' savings; rather, foreigners are begging the United States to take their savings as de facto financing for the production of the goods and services that they are selling to us. This is certainly not the best outcome for the global economy, but the shame of it all is not only that we are consuming too much, but also that the rest of the world is manifestly consuming less than it could or should.

WHAT CAN GO WRONG: BUDGET DEFICITS

On most everyone's list of things to worry about, the federal budget deficit is pretty close to the bottom. That is why budget deficits could end up being a problem in the not too distant future—the 2020s. If the deficit is not seen as a problem, as it was in the 1980s, it will not be dealt with and that delay is what could make it a bigger problem later.

But the 2020s are too far off for most politicians to worry about. And traders and professional money managers are not worried, either, even if they tell you that they know all the tricks that are played with the deficit numbers.

The fear of budget deficits was real in the 1980s, when they reached record highs as a percentage of the gross domestic product (GDP) and economists and politicians argued about the threats of crowding out and inflation.

Budget deficits soaked up a portion of the pool of savings that otherwise would be available for private sector investing. So crowding out meant that borrowing by the government was raising interest rates and preventing private investors from borrowing to invest in new plants and equipment. That crowding out of private investment, in turn, hurt the prospects for long-term economic growth and worker productivity.

Inflation was a threat if there were deficits during a period of strong growth, and the Fed decided to accommodate—or monetize—the red ink. If the central bank did this by pumping more money into the economy to offset the upward pressure on interest rates from the government borrowing, large deficits could have created inflationary pressures by overstimulating the economy.

Although budget deficits began to shrink a little from their record highs of the mid-1980s, they began growing again at the end of the decade, threatening to reach new highs in both dollar terms and as a percentage of economic output. By the election of 1992, when that year's $290 billion budget deficit was back up to 4.7 percent of the gross domestic product, deficits were a driving force behind President Clinton's decision to concentrate on reducing them as a way to bring interest rates down to spur economic growth. For the Clinton administration, there was a direct link between deficits and interest rates.

But in today's Washington, all the concern about deficits has evaporated, although the strong economic growth at the end of the 1990s came as deficits were being reduced and, finally, turned to budget surpluses.

One reason Washington is not worrying about budget deficits today is that the link connecting deficits, the bond market, and higher interest rates is broken. This is because the Federal Reserve has the credibility necessary to convince the bond market that inflation will not become a problem. If inflation is not a problem, then deficits cannot easily become a problem that politicians will think will drive interest rates and inflation higher.

Another reason that Washington does not worry about budget deficits is that there is no point, because Republicans and Democrats remain deadlocked on how to reduce them.

In the bond market, inflation, the pace of economic growth, and whether the Fed is raising rates, cutting rates, or standing still are what set the tone for interest rates. The impact of the budget deficit, traders say, is minimal. Bond traders start with the presumption that the Fed is in the driver's seat—that Fed policy makers have the ability to slow demand, such as the spending by consumers and businesses, and, therefore, neutralize any speedup to demand from budget deficits that they think is too fast.

Many economists believe the threat of budget deficits is exaggerated. Budget deficits, to be sure, can be too big and they can put upward pressure on interest rates. But that textbook stuff should not become a cult or a religion because deficits can be benign and, at times, very beneficial, they argue. Budget deficits are the essence of the Keynesian doctrine, which uses them gladly when the economy is slumping or in recession to help restore growth. In this case, budget deficits stand in for the private sector when its animal spirits cannot generate the oomph the economy needs.

While crowding out of private investment could still be a problem, it is much less of one than it was in the past. This is because the crowding out argument had presumed there was a fixed supply of domestic savings. But with a global economy there is a much larger supply of savings for the government to borrow from, which weakens the crowding out argument.

Nor can you make the assumption, automatically, that deficits mean the government is too big. The government does a great deal of investing. It builds roads and schools and funds education, which, broadly speaking, is an investment in children that will pay off over time. There are also the research and technology that come out of the defense budget. Investing in corporate America is funded with debt, so why cannot government investing be funded with debt?

Economists also argue that it is not the dollar size of the budget deficit that matters. It is the deficit's size in relation to the economy that counts. And that is not a problem right now. Based on the budget totals for fiscal year 2006, which ended September 30, 2006, the deficit of $248 billion was just 1.9 percent of the gross domestic product. That is way down from a record 6 percent of the gross domestic product in 1983 (when the budget deficit's dollar size was $207.8 billion). And that 1.9 percent is comfortably below the 3 percent threshold that worries some economists. The budget deficit just needs to be small enough to stabilize the ratio between it and the gross domestic product, which means if the economy is growing the deficit can grow.

Adding to this deficits-don't-bother-me attitude, especially in Washington, are the official projections of Congress's Congressional Budget Office (CBO). Because of the way deficit projections must be calculated, assuming current law, they show a sharp drop in fiscal year 2012, when the projected deficit falls to $54 billion, or just 0.3 percent of the projected gross domestic product, from $227 billion in 2011 and $328 billion in 2010.[2] But the reason for this sudden drop, as can be seen in Table 3.1, is only that the two big tax cuts passed in President George W. Bush's first term expire under current law, adding billions of dollars of revenue back into the government's coffers. Yet, how likely is Congress and a new president to let these tax cuts be fully repealed? Extending both tax cuts adds $245 billion to the 2012 fiscal year deficit, according to the Congressional Budget Office.

The other troubling projection is that starting in 2019 the Social Security payroll tax will no longer cover the annual benefits

TABLE 3.1 The Declining Budget Deficit: Will It Really Continue to Shrink?

	2005	2006	2007	2008	2009	2010	2011	2012	2013	2014	2015	2016	Total 2007–2011	Total 2007–2016
Total revenues	2,154	2,403	2,515	2,672	2,775	2,890	3,156	3,398	3,555	3,733	3,922	4,118	14,007	32,733
Total outlays	2,472	2,663	2,801	2,945	3,079	3,217	3,382	3,451	3,631	3,797	3,979	4,211	15,425	34,494
Total deficit (−) or surplus	−318	−260	−286	−273	−304	−328	−227	−54	−76	−64	−56	−93	−1,418	−1,761
On-budget	−493	−437	−471	−478	−526	−567	−481	−318	−346	−340	−333	−369	−2,522	−4,228
Off-budget*	175	177	185	204	221	239	254	264	270	275	277	276	1,104	2,466
Effect on the deficit of an extension of the two tax cuts from Bush's first term[†]	0	0	−3	−3	−3	−9	−145	−245	−269	−279	−289	−301	−164	−1,546
Increase in government borrowing costs because of the larger deficits		0				−1	−4	−14	−26	−41	−56	−72	−6	−214

The baseline budget projections of the Congressional Budget Office and how much the extension of the two tax cuts from Bush's first term would add to the budget deficit. The off-budget component of the deficit shows how much the Social Security surplus is reducing the deficit and gives an indication of how much the deficit could rise once that surplus disappears, beginning in 2019.

*Off-budget surpluses comprise surpluses in the Social Security trust funds as well as the net cash flow of the Postal Service.

[†]A minus means an increase in the deficit.

Source: Congressional Budget Office, Joint Committee on Taxation.

paid out by Social Security. (The payroll tax is called FICA, the abbreviation for the Federal Insurance Contributions Act, which placed the taxing provisions for Social Security into the Internal Revenue Code in 1939.)

At this point, there are no more accounting tricks to help reduce the official federal budget deficit, which has been the case for years: Without diverting payroll taxes from Social Security to pay for current spending, the deficit in 2006 would have been $437 billion, instead of the reported $248 billion. As a percentage of the gross domestic product, the $437 billion deficit would have equaled 3.3 percent, above the 3 percent threshold economists worry about.

"Beginning in 2019, annual outlays for Social Security are projected to exceed revenues," according to the Congressional Budget Office.[3] "At that time, the Social Security system will no longer, on net, offset a portion of the deficit in the rest of the budget but instead will increase the total deficit (or reduce the total surplus, if one materializes). Even if spending ends up being lower than expected and revenues are higher than expected, a gap between the two is likely to remain for the indefinite future."

In the same report, the CBO projects that as baby boomers retire the costs of Social Security will rise dramatically, and by the year 2030 spending on Social Security alone will rise to more than 6 percent of the gross domestic product, twice the maximum size the entire deficit should be in relationship to the entire economy.

In its budget update in August 2006, the CBO added that the costs of Medicare and Medicaid will add pressure on the government to find a solution: "The percentage of the population age 65 or older will continue to increase (from 14 percent in 2016 to more than 19 percent in 2030). In addition, health care costs are likely to keep growing faster than GDP, as they have over the past four decades,"[4] which is why Social Security benefits and the rest of the deficit will grow as a percentage of the gross domestic product in the years ahead.

"As a result," the report continues, "spending for Social Security, Medicare, and Medicaid will exert pressures on the budget that economic growth alone is unlikely to alleviate. Consequently, substantial reductions in the projected growth of spending and perhaps a sizable increase in taxes as a share of the economy will probably be necessary to maintain fiscal stability in the coming decades." Without such action, deficits get larger.

These projected figures have changed since this book was finished, but the story they tell is the same: The deficits out there, assuming political reality, are much larger than they appear and any projected surpluses are illusory. So the question is: How threatening are they? Well, this is a point on which we, the two authors, have a disagreement.

McCulley is more sanguine about the future than Fuerbringer. Both agree there is no problem now. In the future, McCulley has confidence that the White House and the Congress will eventually find a solution to the Social Security problem, including Medicare. When the threat of deficits too big to handle, now hidden behind accounting and assumption gimmicks, comes closer, McCulley does not think the bond market will be spooked because it already knows the truth. Instead, the stark numbers, he believes, will finally spook politicians enough to change the political dynamic, leading to approval of the spending cuts and tax increases (including means testing of Social Security) needed to pay for both Social Security and Medicare. Fuerbringer is less confident that the government will do enough fast enough to avoid a run-up in interest rates once the bond market decides to focus on the issue.

If you look at the bond market these days you would agree with McCulley. At the end of 2006, the yield on the Treasury's 10-year note was 4.71 percent while the yield on the Treasury's 30-year bond was 4.81 percent. With the Fed's short-term interest rate benchmark at 5.25 percent, these were not yields that reflected any worry about deficits looming in the future, much less inflation. And this lack of concern, as reflected in interest rates, is there even though those trading in the bond market must know what lies ahead on deficits.

One reason for this lack of concern is that professional investors in the stock market and the bond market do not really have long-term views. They do not look 10 or 20 years ahead. They do not calculate the value of the 30-year bond over 30 years or the value of the 10-year note over 10 years. Their views on value—on whether to buy or sell—are shaped more by what they think of the current expectations of other stock and bond market participants and how those expectations, or perceptions, might change over the next three to five years.

SURPLUS THOUGHTS

It may seem futile right now, but just in case the United States gets back to the point where strong economic growth and good fiscal management bring on the prospect of budget surpluses, here is what we think about that turn of events.

Bond managers come in many religious stripes, but at the office they all believe that fiscal deficits are the raw material for inflationary binges, because they will lead to excessive money creation by the Fed to accommodate the deficits (which is known as monetizing the deficit). Therefore, budget surpluses are as good as budget deficits are bad, because surpluses free the Fed to focus exclusively on keeping inflation low. In addition, the resulting reduction in the issuance of government debt makes more room for the issuance of productivity-enhancing, inflation-retarding private investment.

It is hard to argue with those tenets, but government surpluses do cause problems—enough, in fact, that a small deficit might be better than a large surplus.

The most obvious downside with surpluses is that the credit quality of the stock of all public and private debt will decline. This would happen because the top-quality government bills, notes, and bonds issued by the Treasury would slowly disappear. And as they do, lower-rated private sector debt would become a larger part of the overall debt pool, and therefore the average credit rating would fall.

(Continued)

SURPLUS THOUGHTS *(Continued)*

Like it or not, this means that investors would be adding a little more risk to their fixed-income portfolios. Homework for both money managers and individual investors would be more arduous, because it is more difficult to make decisions about debt that has lower credit ratings.

This does not mean, however, that private sector debt would be less attractive than government debt for your portfolios. In fact, investors who take on more private sector bonds would be getting paid a little more than in the past for adding this extra risk to their portfolios. That is because the yield pickup, or premium, for taking added credit risk would be higher in a world of budget surpluses than in one of budget deficits.

With regard to monetary policy, surpluses should not be a big problem for its operational aspects. But surpluses could change how fast the Fed would have to cut interest rates in the face of an economic downturn.

In a world of budget surpluses, the economy would lose the automatic stabilizing function of the budget deficit. Private sector capital formation is inherently procyclical—it grows as the economic cycle is in an upswing. But government finances, and the government's budget deficit, are inherently countercyclical, increasing as the economy is in a downswing.

A rising deficit in a recession is a very good thing, particularly when it happens automatically. The deficit replaces some of the income lost in the private sector through government benefit programs. Because a growing deficit has to be covered by the issuance of more Treasury bills, notes, and bonds, it also provides default-free obligations for a weakened banking system to buy as private sector credit demand weakens and defaults rise.

In a world of budget surpluses, government debt creation in a recession would not start until the recession created a cyclical deficit, even as private sector capital formation plummeted.

Thus, the automatic stabilizer function of deficits would kick in only with a lag. That may not sound like a problem, but it could be. Congress could move quickly with some combination of tax cuts and additional spending to turn the surplus to a deficit, adding stimulus to the economy. But Congress is not always good at acting in anticipation of a recession. It is not preemptive, like the Fed can be at times. Rather, Congress tends to respond quickly to actual evidence of macroeconomic distress. Thus, in a world of fiscal surpluses, the Federal Reserve will need to be more, not less, preemptive in cutting interest rates when a recession looms on the horizon.

A swing from budget deficits to budget surpluses would also have an impact on the dollar, making a decline when the American economy is weak faster or sharper—or both—than it would have been in a time of regular budget deficits.

Global private sector demand for dollar assets would likely take on an even more distinct procyclical character in a world of fiscal surpluses, in which riskier private sector bonds would become a much larger portion of the stock of debt. And foreign central banks would likely be less eager to play a stabilizing role on the downside, given the relative shortage of higher-rated government notes and bonds for recycling their dollars. This implies that the U.S. dollar would itself become more volatile as momentum-driven foreign private investors rush into and out of it as if it were a high-beta stock.

A world of fiscal surpluses also implies that the dollar would be likely to depreciate in value faster over the long term.

A more volatile dollar and one declining more quickly over the long term would also add to inflation pressures here, as imports from abroad become more expensive as the value of the dollar falls. This extra inflationary pressure could make the Fed hesitant to ease aggressively at the threat of a recession, even as the loss of the automatic stabilizer of a fiscal deficit would argue that Fed should do exactly that.

But no lesser person than Alan Greenspan thinks that the bond market should be paying attention to the budget deficit problem that is out there.

First there are the costs of Social Security and Medicare. The former Fed chairman thinks that the government has already committed itself to a level of medical care in the years ahead that it cannot afford, based on comments made during the interview at PIMCO's Client Conference in March 2006.

Besides the hard dollar calculations of costs, Greenspan is also worried about the way the government forecasts future budget deficits, because these calculations do not assume that the size of the budget deficit could push interest rates higher, which could start a self-feeding process that would lead to even bigger deficits.

"While short-term deficits have no effect that we can find on interest rates, longer-term deficits do—and quite significantly," he said. But he said that deficit forecasts will not reflect this because the official data published by the White House's Office of Management and the Congressional Budget Office assume a constant or flat interest rate. This means there is no assumption that bigger deficits would push interest rates higher than they would have been, raise the government's borrowing costs, and, in turn, increase the size of the budget deficit.

When he was at the Federal Reserve, Greenspan said central bank economists added assumptions of such a potential feedback to deficit forecasts. And what they showed, he said, is that it is not hard "to go down a slippery slope where interest rates begin to rise inordinately, interest payments become very large, and, therefore, the deficits become large, which causes interest rates to go up still more, which causes interest payments to go, et cetera, and it's an unstable system."

In conclusion, Greenspan wondered when the bond market would begin taking account of the budget deficit risks that are out there (that is, when it would start pushing interest rates higher). He was mystified enough to call this his newest conundrum, the same word he used when he said it was very difficult to explain why longer-term interest rates did not rise in 2004 and

2005, even though the Fed was pushing short-term rates higher and higher.

"We are talking potentially real concerns out there," he said, referring to the fact that investors buying 30-year bonds now at very low yields do not appear to realize that they are taking on deficit risk in the decades ahead without being compensated for it. "When does discounting begin?" he asked. "You buy a 30-year issue now—you are buying a big chunk of that out there. That is my next conundrum."

There is nothing investors can do about the potential deficit problem now. It is often true in investing that even when you anticipate a problem correctly, there is not much you can do about it in advance, if most investors have decided not to worry about it for now. In fact, acting too early can be a big mistake. So, in the case of budget deficits, it will have to be wait and see, and be ready to act.

WHAT CAN GO WRONG: BUBBLES

Capitalism is a going concern that from time to time needs financial markets to be unruly, or even irrational, for the system to work properly. In other words, financial bubbles are normal.

But three conditions mean that bubbles are likely to become a more regular feature of the financial landscape and more inevitable than ever: a long period of price stability, which whets the appetite for risk because investors think financial markets are safer than they really are; the fact that capital is allocated through the market price of interest rates, making the Federal Reserve's job of controlling the availability of capital much more difficult; and the Fed's unwillingness to step in to restrain or prick bubbles.

Investors are familiar with the last two financial bubbles, the housing bubble that popped sometime in 2006 and the stock market bubble, which burst in 2000. The stock market bubble made a lot of people rich, and a lot of people—the late arrivals—much poorer. Smaller investors made up a large percentage of the losers because they are often the last to be swept up by a bubble's euphoria. The damage from the housing bubble is still being sorted out.

What makes bubbles a serious threat is that the damage they can cause after they burst may not be easily containable, which could lead to a sharp recession and the threat of deflation.

What many investors may not know is how big a role the Federal Reserve played in creating these bubbles and how unwilling the central bank was to do anything to restrain the stock bubble, even when policy makers knew it was a threat.

How bubbles develop in the years ahead will depend a lot on whether the Fed, under its new leadership, will take its own steps and encourage government and financial regulators to work with the central bank, either to make bubbles less likely or to deal with them when they are first spotted so they would wreak less financial havoc than when they are allowed to burst on their own.

Ben S. Bernanke, the new chairman of the Federal Reserve, has given some indications that he does not want to leave bubbles to their own devices. But he has yet to be tested. If he decides to go in this direction, there might be hope of some guidance from the Fed for investors, including warnings that this or that financial cooker is getting too hot.

But Alan Greenspan is the big figure in the recent history of bubbles. In an uncharitable view, he can be seen as a fan. Later we will show how he created the housing bubble as a way to finance consumer spending and to keep the economy on its feet while corporate America was in the dumps in the wake of the stock market crash and the corporate scandals that followed.

Or if he was not a fan, he did decide that nothing could be done about bubbles, except to clean up after them as best a central bank could. And the problem with that strategy is that it just may encourage more bubbles.

No less an authority than Greenspan confirms the outlook for more bubbles in the future and why that is, noting that the Fed's own success in reining in inflation and smoothing out the economic cycle is one reason the inevitable is more inevitable.

"In perhaps what must be the greatest irony of economic pol-icymaking, success at stabilization carries its own risks," Greenspan said in the text of his remarks to the annual meeting of the National Association for Business Economics in Chicago in September 2005. "Monetary policy—in fact, all economic pol-icy—to the extent that it is successful over a prolonged period, will reduce economic variability and, hence, perceived credit risk and interest rate term premiums."[5] Without using the world *bub-ble*—but being very clear about what he meant—he concluded that "history cautions that extended periods of low concern about credit risk have invariably been followed by reversal, with an attendant fall in the prices of risky assets." In other words, the bubble bursts.

Despite his penchant to obscure what he means in a lot of economic-speak and jargon, Greenspan makes a convincing argu-ment for what the era of relative economic stability he helped en-gineer means for bubbles. So let him make the case for more bubbles ahead.

In testimony to Congress in July 2005, Greenspan was ex-plaining why the yield on the Treasury's 10-year note was so sur-prisingly low despite the Fed's move to raise its short-term interest rate target, the federal funds rate, by 2.25 percentage points to 3.25 percent over the previous year. That was his "co-nundrum." The yield on the 10-year note was actually half of a percentage point lower in July 2005 (4.2 percent) than it was be-fore the short-term rate increases began in June 2004 (4.7 per-cent). One reason, Greenspan said, was the willingness of investors to take on more risk, which resulted in the lowering of term premiums in the Treasury and other fixed-income markets. Term premiums reflect the fact that investors want to be paid more to lend money over a longer period of time. So, usually the interest rate on the Treasury's 10-year note is higher than the in-terest rate of securities with shorter maturities, like the five-year note or the two-year note.

Greenspan argued that the surprising fall in the yield on the 10-year Treasury note was due to a decline in this so-called term premium. "Such estimates," he said, "are subject to considerable uncertainty. Nevertheless, they suggest that risk takers have been encouraged by a perceived increase in economic stability to reach out to more distant time horizons. These actions have been accompanied by significant declines in measures of expected volatility in equity and credit markets inferred from prices of stock and bond options and narrow credit risk premiums. History cautions that long periods of relative stability often engender unrealistic expectations of its permanence and, at times, may lead to financial excess and economic stress."[6]

Greenspan provided a nice conclusion to this thought in comments he made at the symposium sponsored by the Federal Reserve Bank of Kansas City in Jackson Hole, Wyoming, in August 2005.

> *The lowered risk premiums—the apparent consequence of a long period of economic stability—coupled with greater productivity growth have propelled asset prices higher. The rising prices of stocks, bonds, and, more recently, of homes, have engendered a large increase in the market value of claims which, when converted to cash, are a source of purchasing power. Financial intermediaries, of course, routinely convert capital gains in stocks, bonds, and homes into cash for businesses and households to facilitate purchase transactions. The conversions have been markedly facilitated by the financial innovation that has greatly reduced the cost of such transactions.*
>
> *Thus, this vast increase in the market value of asset claims is in part the indirect result of investors accepting lower compensation for risk. Such an increase in market value is too often viewed by market participants as structural and permanent. To some extent, those higher values may be reflecting the increased flexibility and resilience of our economy. But what they perceive as newly abundant liquidity can readily disappear. Any onset of increased investor caution elevates risk premiums and, as a consequence, lowers asset values and promotes the liquidation of the debt that supported higher asset prices. This is the reason that history*

has not dealt kindly with the aftermath of protracted periods of low risk premiums.[7]

But Greenspan had no interest in having the Fed do anything about a bubble, even when policy makers saw it coming. He made that clear in his remarks to the annual meeting of the National Association for Business Economics in September 2005:

Relying on policy makers to perceive when speculative asset bubbles have developed and then to implement timely policies to address successfully these misalignments in asset prices is simply not realistic. As the Federal Open Market Committee (FOMC) transcripts of the mid-1990s duly note, we at the Fed were uncomfortable with a stock market that appeared as early as 1996 to disconnect from its moorings.

Yet the significant monetary tightening of 1994 did not prevent what must by then have been the beginnings of the bubble of the 1990s. And equity prices continued to rise during the tightening of policy between mid-1999 and May 2000. Indeed, the equity market's ability to withstand periods of tightening arguably reinforced the bull market's momentum. The FOMC knew that tools were available to choke off the stock market boom, but those tools would only have been effective if they undermined market participants' confidence in future stability. Market participants, however, read the resilience of the economy and stock prices in the face of monetary tightening as an indication of undiscounted market strength.

By the late 1990s, it appeared to us that very aggressive action would have been required to counteract the euphoria that developed in the wake of extraordinary gains in productivity growth spawned by technological change. In short, we would have needed to risk precipitating a significant recession, with unknown consequences. The alternative was to wait for the eventual exhaustion of the forces of boom. We concluded that the latter course was by far the safer. Whether that judgment continues to hold up through time has yet to be determined.[8]

This hands-off policy is disturbing because it makes bubbles more likely. Investors—especially speculators—like to push the envelope when they are playing a market trend, like the stock market in the 1990s when it appeared "to disconnect from its moorings" or when the housing market, also in Greenspan's words, showed some "signs of froth"[9] in 2005.

If there were a threat to those kinds of trends continuing, it would be harder for investors to pile on, which is what happens when a bubble is being inflated. The other side of the Fed policy, mopping up after a bubble does burst, also seems to help bubble formation because the Fed has promised lots of help to stabilize things after a bubble implodes.

The current environment of stable and low inflation and low interest rates is the reason for this promised cleanup and is another of those pesky negatives resulting from the otherwise extremely successful effort by the Fed to bring inflation into line.

Federal Reserve policy makers are worried that an economic slowdown triggered by a bubble bursting could lead to a sharp drop in the rate of inflation. And with inflation as low as it is—2.2 percent for the 12 months through November 2006, using the price index for personal consumption expenditures, excluding food and energy—the economy is not far from falling into deflation, when prices are actually falling. That is an economic turn of events that no one wants. The cost is great: the death of animal-spirited risk taking, innovation, technological advancement, and productivity growth and the risk of declining living standards. And once there, getting out, as Japan has proved, can be excruciatingly difficult.

Consequently, investors, especially speculators, expect that if inflation is low and in check, a bursting bubble will elicit a much larger and faster reduction in interest rates from the Federal Reserve than there would be if inflation were higher and there were no deflationary threat. And that makes them willing to take on even more risk because they feel there is a safety net under them.

There have been hints on how the post-Greenspan Fed might handle bubbles from Bernanke, who took over as chairman in

February 2006. In Bernanke's first speech as a governor of the Federal Reserve in 2002, he had argued that financial deregulation, done poorly, has helped spawn financial bubbles in the past.

> *During recent decades, unsustainable increases in asset prices have been associated on a number of occasions with botched financial liberalization, in both emerging-market and industrialized countries. The typical pattern is that lending institutions are given substantially expanded powers that are not matched by a commensurate increase in regulatory supervision (think of the savings and loans in the United States in the 1980s). A situation develops in which institutions can directly or indirectly take speculative positions using funds protected by the deposit insurance safety net—the classic "heads I win, tails you lose" situation.*
>
> *When this moral hazard is present, credit flows rapidly into inelastically supplied assets, such as real estate. Rapid appreciation is the result, until the inevitable albeit belated regulatory crackdown stops the flow of credit and leads to an asset-price crash. Bubbles of this type may be identifiable to some extent after they have begun, but the right policy is to do the financial deregulation correctly—that is, in a way that does not allow speculative misuse of the safety net—in the first place. Or failing that, to intervene and fix the problem when it is recognized.*[10]

But as a cure, Bernanke rejected bubble popping by the central bank. Although he said that it would be nice to find ways to reduce the occurrences of financial bubbles, he said the central bank's monetary policy tools are not designed for this kind of repair work. "Even putting aside the great difficulty of identifying bubbles in asset prices, monetary policy cannot be directed finely enough to guide asset prices without risking severe collateral damage to the economy," he said in the same speech.

Instead, Bernanke favors micro-level, rather than macro-level, policies, including assurance of proper capital adequacy in the banking system, stress-testing of bank portfolios to ensure they have not taken on too much risk, more financial disclosure and financial transparency, improved financial education for investors, better planning and scrutiny of future financial liberalizations, and a willingness by the central bank to be the lender of last resort, when needed.

One micro-level tool that is not on this list should also be considered for use against bubbles. It is the raising of margin requirements. Margin is the portion of the cost of securities that investors have to put up to borrow the rest of the money to buy securities. It is currently 50 percent for each purchase, and there is a maintenance margin of at least 25 percent. Raising these levels obviously would discourage the purchase of stocks on borrowed money or, in Wall Street jargon, leverage, which is the high-octane fuel for a market bubble.

A return to Greenspan's own words shows the role he played in the nurturing of the stock bubble of the 1990s and how he waffled on the effectiveness of margin requirements as a bubble deflator.

Greenspan introduced the words "irrational exuberance" to the financial lexicon on December 5, 1996, in a speech to the American Enterprise Institute for Public Policy Research in Washington, D.C.:

> Clearly, sustained low inflation implies less uncertainty about the future, and lower risk premiums imply higher prices of stocks and other earning assets. We can see that in the inverse relationship exhibited by price/earnings ratios and the rate of inflation in the past. But how do we know when irrational exuberance has unduly escalated asset values, which then become subject to unexpected and prolonged contractions as they have in Japan over the past decade? And how do we factor that assessment into monetary policy? We as central bankers need not be concerned if a collapsing financial asset bubble does not threaten to impair the real economy, its production, jobs, and price stability. Indeed, the sharp stock market break of 1987 had few nega-

*tive consequences for the economy. But we should not un-
derestimate or become complacent about the complexity of
the interactions of asset markets and the economy. Thus,
evaluating shifts in balance sheets generally, and in asset
prices particularly, must be an integral part of the development of monetary policy.*[11]

Surprisingly, Greenspan's comments had only a muted impact
on the stock market. Stock markets in Germany and Japan fell 3
percent on December 6 after Greenspan's comments, but in the
United States the Dow Jones Industrial Average rebounded in af-
ternoon trading and cut its early-morning 2.2 percent decline by
more than half. The Standard & Poor's 500 stock index slipped
just 4.79 points, or 0.6 percent. And despite further declines in
the days immediately following his remarks, within just two
weeks the Dow had rebounded to back above where it had been
before Greenspan uttered the words "irrational exuberance."

Apologists for Greenspan's subsequent failure to address the
bubbling in stocks always note that he never declared stocks to be
irrationally exuberant in that December speech, but that he
merely mused out loud as to how he would know if they were.
The transcript of the September 24, 1996, meeting of the Federal
Open Market Committee, the policy-making body of the Federal
Reserve, shows that those apologists can no longer apologize.
Some 10 weeks before uttering "irrational exuberance," and with
the Dow Jones Industrial Average at 5,874.03—563 points or almost 9 percent below where it was on December 5—Greenspan
declared to his colleagues:

> *I recognize that there is a stock market bubble problem at
> this point, and I agree with Governor [Lawrence B.] Lindsey
> that this is a problem we should keep an eye on. We have
> very great difficulty in monetary policy when we confront
> stock market bubbles. That is because, to the extent that we
> are successful in keeping product price inflation down, his-
> tory tells us that price-earnings ratios under those conditions*

go through the roof. What is really needed to keep stock market bubbles from occurring is a lot of product price inflation, which historically has tended to undercut stock markets almost everywhere. There is a clear trade-off. If monetary policy succeeds in one, it fails in the other. Now, unless we have the capability of playing in between and managing to know exactly when to push a little here and to pull a little there, it is not obvious to me that there is a simple set of monetary policy solutions that deflate the bubble. We have the possibility of raising major concerns by increasing margin requirements. I guarantee that if you want to get rid of the bubble, whatever it is, that will do it. My concern is that I am not sure what else it will do.[12]

Based on this transcript it is clear that Greenspan had, in fact, already identified a bubble in stocks 10 weeks before his so-called musings on irrational exuberance. So his comments 10 weeks later were not a rhetorical question in search of an answer, but an answer veiled in a rhetorical question. And Greenspan did indeed identify a hike in margin requirements—a micro-level regulatory tool of the sort that the new chairman, Bernanke, may be interested in using—as a guaranteed way to get rid of a bubble. But Greenspan declined to use this tool, for fear that it would work too well.

And just over three years after his comments at the 1996 meeting of the Federal Open Market Committee, Greenspan changed his tune about the effectiveness of a hike in margin requirements as a tool for popping a stock market bubble. In his mind, the margin-requirement tool morphed from a "guaranteed" way to get rid of the bubble in September of 1996 to a tool of no importance in February of 2000, except perhaps to discriminate against small investors, who, he argued, would suffer the most from a change in margin requirements.

Here are his comments during questions and answers before the House Banking Committee on February 17, 2000, according to Bloomberg. The Dow Jones Industrial Average was at 10,514.57, already down 10.3 percent from its then bubble-induced all-time closing high of 11,722.98 in January. The NASDAQ Composite index was at 4,548.92 with still one big spurt to go to its bubble-induced all-time high of 5,048.62 in March.

The problem that I have had with the issue of moving on margins is not concern of what it would do to the market-place; it's the evidence which suggests that it has very little impact on the price structure of the market, or anything else. It has one characteristic, however. It basically has its impact, its incidence on smaller investors, because they have no alternative means of financing. Larger investors have all forms of financing, and margin is a small part of their financing. It is true that there probably are some professional investors who are using margin debt for purposes of various different types of hedging or what-have-you. My impression is that it's probably very small and not an issue that one should be concerned about.

The truth of the matter is that margin debt did, in fact, emerge in 1999 as the helium in the technology bubble. And it was not just small punters breathing the stuff, but men like Bernard J. Ebbers, the former chief executive of WorldCom, who was a leading architect of the bubbles in investment and leverage in the telecom sector that bedeviled the economy for years. He was sentenced to 25 years in jail for the role he played in the fraud that led to WorldCom's collapse.

Some argue that the failure to use the margin requirement does not matter because Greenspan did what was needed by hiking interest rates from 1999 into 2000, which did deflate the stock bubble. At some philosophical level, this is correct. But at the practical level, it is not. It makes no sense for the Federal Reserve to eschew using a micro-level regulatory tool against a bubble when the consequence of refusing to use this tool is to generate unnecessary volatility in the Fed's macro interest rate tool, the fed funds rate.

Which brings us to the matter of a bubble in the U.S. residential housing market, a bubble that Greenspan and the Fed participated in forming much more aggressively than they did the stock market bubble.

The housing bubble, of course, did not start off as a bubble. It was, in fact, medicine for a sick economy after the stock market bubble burst and U.S. corporations were turning inward, cutting capital spending and working to repair their balance sheets, after stretching them to the limit, and beyond, at the end of the 1990s.

Capitalism in America is alive and well as long as it has a game in the casino that can be levered into capital gains that can be spent. Since capital gains from stocks were no longer enough to power the consumer, the Federal Reserve turned to housing, knowing that mortgage refinancing against the rising equity values in homes across the United States would provide a new source of billions of dollars for Americans to spend, as can be seen in Figure 3.2. So Fed policy makers pushed their target for

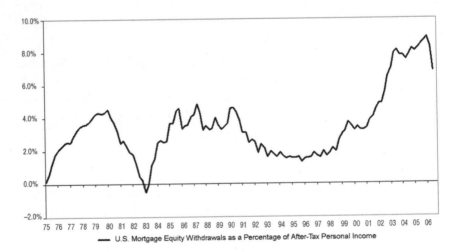

FIGURE 3.2 The Home as ATM

The surge in the money that homeowners took from the equity in their homes when they were refinancing their mortgages helped power the recovery from the 2001 recession.

Source: PIMCO. Data from the Federal Reserve.

the fed funds rate lower; mortgage rates followed, falling to their lowest levels in decades; and home mortgage refinancing took off.

This was the house game and Greenspan was both the croupier and the credit clerk. He would, no doubt, disagree with that description. And, indeed, at the beginning there was no bubble—and the Fed chairman thought a bubble was unlikely, as he made clear in testimony to the Joint Economic Committee of Congress in April 2002:

> The ongoing strength in the housing market has raised concerns about the possible emergence of a bubble in home prices. However, the analogy often made to the building and bursting of a stock price bubble is imperfect. First, unlike in the stock market, sales in the real estate market incur substantial transactions costs and, when most homes are sold, the seller must physically move out. Doing so often entails significant financial and emotional costs and is an obvious impediment to stimulating a bubble through speculative trading in homes. Thus, while stock market turnover is more than 100 percent annually, the turnover of home ownership is less than 10 percent annually—scarcely tinder for speculative conflagration. Second, arbitrage opportunities are much more limited in housing markets than in securities markets. A home in Portland, Oregon, is not a close substitute for a home in Portland, Maine, and the "national" housing market is better understood as a collection of small, local housing markets. Even if a bubble were to develop in a local market, it would not necessarily have implications for the nation as a whole.
>
> These factors certainly do not mean that bubbles cannot develop in house markets and that home prices cannot decline: Indeed, home prices fell significantly in several parts of the country in the early 1990s. But because the turnover of homes is so much smaller than that of stocks and because the underlying demand for living space tends to be revised very gradually, the speed and magnitude of price rises and declines often observed in markets for securities are more difficult to create in markets for homes.[13]

By dismissing bubble worries in April 2002, Greenspan made clear the policy bet he was making: During the rehabilitation of corporate America from its sins of excess in investment and leverage, the American household would be encouraged to bid up the prices of houses, borrow against that rising paper value, and spend the paper capital gains on cars, computers, and many other items to keep the economy perking along.

By the end of his term as chairman nearly four years later, Greenspan would acknowledge some "signs of froth" in housing. But he stuck with the old macro interest rate tool, the federal funds rate, to curb housing's bubble proclivities. The irony of that was that it did not work well, because, as noted earlier, the Fed suddenly had trouble in 2004, 2005, and 2006 in getting the longer-term interest rates that set the prices of mortgages to rise along with its increases in its short-term interest rate target.

Because of Greenspan's interest rate conundrum, he left office with the housing bubble in the hands of his successor, Bernanke. It was Bernanke who had to finish off the housing bubble, and it is Bernanke who will have to deal with its aftermath.

WHAT CAN GO WRONG: RECESSIONS

It can be said that at one time—when inflation was out of control—economic downturns, or recessions, had their value. That is because the decline in growth also was an opportunity to ratchet down the inflation rate.

During the Fed's battle against inflation from October 1979 to May 2003, the Federal Reserve always wanted each cyclical peak and trough in the rate of inflation to be below the prior cyclical peak and trough, as can be seen in Figure 3.3. This strategy even had a formal, fancy name: opportunistic disinflation, which was coined by Laurence H. Meyer, a former governor of the Federal Reserve. What it was all about was waiting for recessions to opportunistically take inflation lower and then to use preemptive rate increases to stave off any increase in the rate of inflation in the subsequent recoveries.

The Federal Reserve was quite comfortable with the notion of the next "opportunistic" recession taking inflation lower, toward the promised land of secular price stability.

But that is no longer the case. The next recession will be inopportune. With the pace of price increases low and in check, the biggest risk facing the economy is not rising inflation, but the chance, albeit small, that a recession or a bursting asset bubble, or both, will shock the economy enough to cause a deflationary spiral.

The closer the inflation rate is to zero, the greater the risk that the downward price pressures that come with the next economic slowdown could tip the country into a bout of deflation. This means that future recessions are more threatening than those in the past.

What is needed to help stave off this threat is a buffer of inflation, a cushion against a fall in prices. That cushion—a slightly higher inflation rate than the Fed would have accepted in the

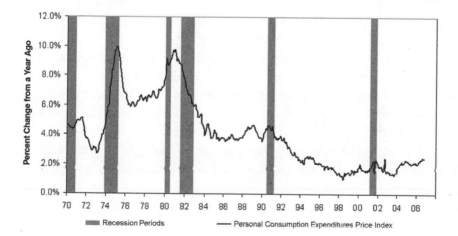

FIGURE 3.3 Opportunistic Disinflation

Taking advantage of the fall in prices during recessions—and keeping a cap on the lower inflation rate after recessions—helped win the war against inflation.

Source: Bureau of Economic Analysis.

past—is necessary so policy makers would not have to cut interest rates so precipitously that they would make investors look beyond the risks of deflation in the financial environment, encouraging irrational exuberance.

How much cushion is needed? That is hard to say. But the 1 percent to 2 percent comfort zone of Fed officials, using the core (excluding food and energy) personal consumption expenditures deflator, the Fed's favorite inflation measure, is too low. We think the Fed needs another full percentage point of protection.

Such a cushion would mean that a cyclical uptick in inflation is not categorically a bad thing and would not mean that investors should conclude that the Fed has gone soft on inflation. But unless financial markets and investors are prepared for this, a market sell-off is possible at the sight of Fed policy makers accepting this extra inflation.

Adding to concerns about the next recession is the fact that it may be very hard to get the economy turned around once it has fallen into a slump.

It was not that difficult to revive the economy after it fell into a recession in March 2001, the first economic slump in a decade.

As noted earlier, by keeping interest rates low, the Fed helped turn homes into ATMs. With mortgage interest rates the lowest in decades, millions of Americans refinanced their mortgages, with most of them turning some of their rising home equity into cash that fueled the consumer spending that pumped up the economy again. The downturn lasted just eight months, less than the 10-month average for recessions since World War II.[14]

But it is difficult to see what sector of the economy can be levered up in the next recession. Housing is not likely to act as a tonic this time. It is going to be a deadweight. With the home ATMs shut down, people will spend less and save more, which would be a big drag on economic growth.

At the end of 2006, there were convincing signs that the economy was slowing. The housing slump had begun. The pace of residential construction was decelerating and housing starts were well below their recent highs. Sales were also falling, and, according to Fed policy makers, other indicators showed that the housing market would slow even further. Some analysts were forecasting a drop in home sales of 20 percent to 30 percent. Although the price of a barrel of crude oil had retreated from its record high, retail sales were the slowest they had been in three years.

A slowdown does not mean a recession, so as this book was finished, the question of when the next recession would begin was still open. But it appeared that the next recession would have post-housing-bubble blues written all over it.

The next U.S. recession is also likely to be hard on the rest of the world, especially emerging markets. When that recession occurs, the rest of the world will have lost its best friend, which is the American consumer, so economic growth will slow globally. Or, to use an old economists' cliché, when the United States sneezes, the world catches a cold. This means the rest of the world's central banks will have to be alert to cutting their own interest rates quickly to try to offset the economic drag from a drop in spending by millions of American consumers.

And when that recession is over there may be a surprise waiting at the other end—a jump in inflation that goes beyond the cushion that we think the Fed needs as a buffer against deflation.

Why? Because it may take a lot of stimulus to get the economy going again and the Fed will have to leave that stimulus spigot open long enough to be sure the economy is back on its feet. This could, however, turn out to be too much extra fuel for growth, setting off new inflationary pressures. We do not fear this at the moment. But we mention it because it is in the forecast of Bill Gross, the chief investment officer at PIMCO and McCulley's boss.

WHAT CAN GO WRONG: CHINA

If it is not too much of an intellectual stretch to say that China is part of the monetary union that is called the United States—the 51st state, if you will—then it is not too much of a stretch to say that what can go wrong is that China decides—or is forced—to secede.

First, the 51st state. As noted earlier, China has kept its currency, the yuan, tied as closely as possible to the value of the U.S. dollar because that makes China's exports more competitive. But in doing this, China has essentially ceded the control of its monetary policy to the Federal Reserve, in the same way that all the 50 states in the United States have.

Here's why.

Both the United States and China have fiat currencies, which are not backed by anything but each sovereign's declaration that they are legal tender for all debts, public and private.

In such fiat currency regimes, the sovereign has the ability to choose one of two goals for its central bank: stabilizing either the domestic purchasing power of the currency or the foreign exchange value of the currency. The sovereign can stabilize the domestic purchasing power of the currency by having its central bank target a domestic price for the currency, which is done by raising or lowering interest rates, or by having the central bank target the quantity of its currency, which is done by having the central bank set a growth rate for the domestic money stock or money supply.

The sovereign can stabilize the foreign exchange value of the currency by having its central bank target the price of the currency in the foreign exchange market, letting currency reserves rise and fall as necessary as a consequence of foreign exchange intervention activities.

What a fiat currency country cannot do is instruct its central bank to use all three possible monetary policy levers: a domestic interest rate, the size of the domestic money stock, and the currency's foreign exchange value.

By the laws of central bank plumbing, a fiat currency country's central bank can peg only one of these three policy targets; once one of the variables is pegged, the other two become market-determined, unless constrained by regulatory structures.

In the United States, the Federal Reserve pegs the domestic price of money—the overnight interest rate between banks that is called the federal funds rate. In turn, growth in the domestic money stock and the foreign exchange value of the dollar all adjust, via market forces, to be consistent with the Fed's chosen peg for the fed funds rate. Accordingly, the United States does not have a currency policy per se, either strong or weak. It has a fed funds policy.

In contrast, China has chosen to give its central bank a target for the foreign exchange value of its currency, pegged to the dollar. This in theory means that China cannot have a target for its domestic short-term interest rate or growth in its domestic money stock. This is not precisely correct, though, because China does not have an unregulated capital market or a fully private domestic banking system. So China, unlike the United States, does retain some degree of control over variables besides the yuan's pegged exchange rate versus the dollar.

But these are technical matters, which should not obscure reality: China does not have an independently determined domestic monetary policy, because China has chosen to peg its currency to the dollar, thereby importing U.S. monetary policy.

This exchange rate tie is part of the mercantilist model China chose to move it along the path from a centrally planned to a market-centered economy.

If a country wants to shift from a centralized economy to a capitalist system, it has to expose what its people can manufacture to a market test. But the country cannot do that at home because it does not have a free market. So it has to see if what its people make will sell in the rest of the world's markets. The country's economy becomes mercantile, focusing its development efforts on exporting abroad, as can be seen in China's case in Figure 3.4.

First the government, through a central bank, fixes the value of its currency at a low exchange rate so that its exports will compete well abroad. Then manufacturers grab market share in the developed world, which has the markets that will test the value of the country's resources—in China's case, labor and savings. As products are sold abroad, the central bank builds up huge reserves

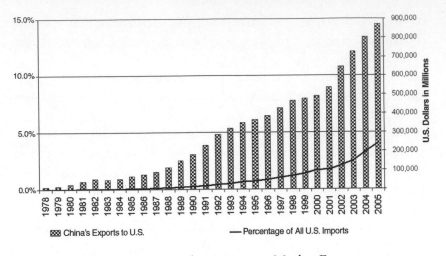

FIGURE 3.4   Export Mania: The Route to a Market Economy
Source: PIMCO. Data from the Bureau of Economic Analysis.

of foreign currency, and they are funneled back to the countries where the products are being sold—in this case, mostly to the United States. So it ends up as a grand vendor financing scheme to finance the goods that are sold abroad.

The fact that the currency is undervalued and the central bank has large dollar reserves gives foreign investors confidence to invest in China. The undervalued currency means foreigners can invest cheaply and hope for big gains when the currency does rise in value. The large reserves mean that China has the wherewithal to keep control over the mercantilist process, if there is no protectionist threat.

So the foreign exchange reserves are effectively acting as collateral for the direct foreign investment, which brings technology and capitalist knowledge. The technology and foreign investment help the country move up the production ladder, making higher valued-added goods at each step up.

Mercantilism reigns in much of Asia, where high domestic savings rates mean a relatively low level of consumer buying at home, huge foreign exchange reserves, undervalued currencies, and large current account surpluses.

This is not the American model. Americans operate on the theory that consumption comes first; hearses don't come with U-Haul trailers, and, therefore, Americans spend accordingly. In Asia, consumption is an afterthought in the pursuit of ever-greater stores of international wealth.

Neither the Asian model nor the Anglo-Saxon model is inherently right or wrong. People's utility functions are not homogeneous: different strokes for different folks. And because people's utility functions are different, there is scope for win-win international trade: We can help each other out, whether willingly or unwillingly, as China has helped us on our current account deficit and we have helped China on its economic development.

Ultimately, though, China will graduate from the American University for the Study of Capitalism. It will switch from a mass production economy to a mass production and mass consumption economy and have the courage and ability to free its exchange rate and shift away from its mercantilist model. So China will secede at some point. In fact, China took a first step in that direction in the summer of 2005 when it revalued the yuan by 2 percent, making it stronger against the dollar, and let it float marginally upward thereafter. That process was accelerated a little in the fall of 2006. These moves came under pressure from the United States, but China has only moved a little, so its special monetary union is still effectively a going concern.

Even if secession is a slow process, interest rates and inflation will be higher than they would be otherwise. As the Chinese currency is allowed to appreciate against the dollar, their goods will become more expensive for Americans, and it is not clear how much competition from other emerging market countries will offset that upward price pressure. And as the yuan appreciates, China's central bank will be selling fewer yuan for dollars, reducing the dollar reserves that are recycled into the U.S. Treasury market. That means interest rates could be higher than otherwise. That is going to be unpleasant for American investors—but it should not be worse than that.

If this is an abrupt process, which could happen under threats of protectionism from the United States, all the above should happen but at a pace that could be quite disruptive to the economy, sending interest rates higher quickly, the dollar down quickly, and inflation higher, and—if the dominos all fall the wrong way—causing a recession. And because China's tie to the dollar is so entwined with helping finance the U.S. current account deficit, the threat of a big disruption from an accelerated secession is greater.

Either way, therefore, it is not much of a stretch to say that China could have a big say over interest rates, inflation, monetary policy, and even the pace of economic growth in the years ahead.

Our belief that this secession can be deliberate and orderly is based on the fact that China cannot leave its mercantilist path or opt out of its currency tie too early because that would destroy its developmental model. China still needs to move slowly toward the free trading of its currency to get all the benefits it wants from its transition to capitalism.

There is the threat that protectionism could force China to untie from its dollar anchor a lot faster. While Americans have not been ardently protectionist for some time, the idea of retaliation against China has been gaining ground. One big threat, a trade bill sponsored by Senator Charles E. Schumer, a New York Democrat, and Senator Lindsey Graham, a South Carolina Republican, was pulled back in the fall of 2006 after China indicated that it was slightly speeding up its divorce from the dollar. But the threat will remain because the Schumer-Graham trade bill had gotten China's attention, and it is not yet clear if the secession process is moving fast enough for politicians like Schumer and Graham.

Protectionism also remains a threat because it is an attractive strategy for a politician from a vote-getting point of view. The cost of protectionism can often be spread very lightly among millions of American consumers. For example, consumers pay more for sugar because of protectionism, but that is not making them single-issue voters against the politicians who support the quotas. Only the sugar worker is going to be a single-issue voter for that politician. In the case of China, we think the cost of a sudden policy swerve will be much more severe for millions of American consumers, but it is still not likely to turn these consumers against a few politicians.

Assuming we do not get an escalation of protectionism, China will do the unwinding of the yuan in its own time frame, on the installment plan. And that will be to the benefit of the United States because it should help bring the current account deficit down to a manageable, not just a sustainable, level, without a big economic disruption.

There are, of course, other things that can go wrong with China. One of them is happening right now. It is the price of oil and it is sapping growth potential in the United States.

The path of economic development for China and other emerging market countries means that demand for energy is growing faster than supply, which naturally leads to an increase in the real price. In addition, that higher price transfers more wealth to oil producers, many of whom do not like the United States. The situation could end up in fisticuffs.

In the long run, the world needs the real price of energy to go up enough to encourage conservation efforts and the development of alternative forms of energy. That way, everything works out—eventually.

The flip side is a roller-coaster ride on which you get nasty spikes in oil prices that are destabilizing to the economy and to the geopolitical stability of the world. Spikes do not help create conservation and energy alternatives. You need a steady higher price to encourage conservation. Investors cannot deal with the price of oil whizzing about by $15 a barrel all the time.

The flip side is with us right now. It is the consequence of China's development plan, and so far it is not working out the way that it should. It is not making us—the United States—conserve and create energy alternatives.

4

Reading the Federal Reserve

The art of observing the nation's central bank is not an everyday job or requirement, except for those professionals, like Paul Mc-Culley, who get paid to do it. But for all investors it's worthwhile to know more about the Federal Reserve.

The reason is that the Fed often has more to say about your investments than anybody else. Federal Reserve policy makers are the ones who change the route of your investment path. They are the ones who alter investment straightaways, when a portfolio could be on autopilot, to investment curves.

In today's environment, navigating a curve means moving money around in your portfolio. While we are still interested in promoting long-term investing, better overall returns can be achieved—or losses avoided—by skillful adjustments when the Fed is redrawing the investing road map.

In this chapter we tell you how to read what the Federal Reserve is doing and how to anticipate its next move. We also show you how to get a sense of what the market thinks the Fed is going to do next.

We explain what the Fed does operationally to promote economic growth and fight inflation and how difficult that job can be. We tell you when the Fed really became independent and review a few of the other big moments in Fed history. And we look at the rest of the world's central banks to show you that Fed policy is no longer the sole straw stirring the global monetary policy drink.

CURVES AHEAD

There are many ways to read the Federal Reserve. You can parse every speech of the chairman of the Fed and every statement put out by the Federal Open Market Committee. You can just believe in the Fed, which means you expect that policy makers will tame inflation and prevent deflation. Or you can take some position in between.

But even if you are a believer and confident that the Fed will beat inflation or deflation, you do not know what route Fed policy makers will take to get there. You do not know how high they will raise or how low they will cut interest rates or how long either cycle will take.

And even if those who parse the Fed's every sentence are right about how much higher or lower the Fed is going to move interest rates and how quickly that will happen, they do not know how these actions will go down in the financial markets. Markets may not react the way Fed policy makers or analysts expect. And that means the Fed may have to alter its policy course in an unexpected way.

Reading the Fed, therefore, is still difficult, despite all the changes in the past two decades that have made the nation's central bank much more transparent about what it is doing and thinking. So to start out, we will point investors to a beacon of Fed policy. It is not surefire. But it gives a pretty good indication of when there might be curves ahead.

The guide is the manufacturing index reported monthly by the Institute for Supply Management. The ISM calls it the PMI (Purchasing Managers' Index), based on the ISM's former name, the National Association of Purchasing Managers. (But veteran Wall Street analysts knew it colloquially as the "napalm" index, from the initials for the old name, NAPM.)

Tracking the fed funds rate against the monthly PMI data, as shown in Figure 4.1, shows that since 1987 the Fed has never kept tightening once the PMI dropped below 50. And the Fed has never kept easing once the PMI has topped 55.

The PMI works because the business cycle is, in the end, all about manufacturing, even though manufacturing represents an ever-smaller share of our nation's gross domestic product. There is a simple reason for this: Manufacturing is where the sun rises and sets on the inventory cycle, so the cyclical swings in manufacturing, as reflected in the PMI, are a great proxy for the inventory cycle. And the inventory cycle is what the business cycle is all

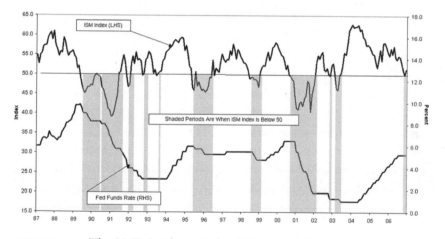

FIGURE 4.1   The PMI Guide to Federal Reserve Policy

Since 1987, Fed policy makers have not kept tightening once the PMI has dropped below 50. They have usually not kept easing once the PMI has risen above 55.

Source: PIMCO data from the Institute for Supply Management and the Federal Reserve.

about: the never-ending balancing act between customers' orders and producers' ability to meet those orders. A surprise on orders, positive or negative, has long ripple effects, exposing inventory levels that are either too high or too low and prices that are either too high or too low.

There is noise on the straightaways. But in the curves, as can be seen in Figure 4.1, the prescience of the PMI in calling the inventory cycle and, with a lag, a change in the Fed's interest rate policy, is clear. The clincher is that the PMI data is available much earlier than good numbers on inventories, making it a perfect leading indicator.

The PMI can be found at the web site of the Institute for Supply Management, at www.ism.ws/. Once there, click on the monthly Manufacturing ISM Report on Business. The PMI report is there. You can also find the history of the PMI on the web site.

How can this help an investor? Since the PMI is a pretty good forecaster of the curves ahead, it can be an indicator of when money might be moved around in a portfolio. As we will show in more detail in Chapter 8, the PMI can be a signal to move money from bonds into stocks or from one part of the bond market to another. A signal that interest rates are about to fall is obviously a good time to move money from bonds into stocks. But even if the PMI is signaling that the Fed is about to raise interest rates, it could be a good idea to take money out of bonds and put them into stocks. In what may be a surprise to some investors, such a move would allow you to pick up the better returns to be had in stocks, based on recent history. So the PMI could signal a good time for investors who want to add risk to their portfolio to move money from fixed income into equities.

Just a word of caution about reading the PMI: Do not try to outanticipate it. McCulley himself missed a call on the PMI index in the spring and summer of 2005, not because the index gave the wrong signal but rather because he saw the PMI index inch close to 50 and decided it was headed below 50, which was the signal that the Fed would stop tightening. He wanted to be ahead of the crowd, but in this case he anticipated too much. The index did slip to 51.4 in May, but then it rebounded in June and did not breach the 50 level in 2005. It did dip below 50 in November 2006 but then popped back above 50 in December.

The way to watch what Fed policy makers are doing is to look at their web site, at www.federalreserve.gov. Here an investor can find all the official statements and reports on monetary policy and all the speeches and testimony of Federal Reserve officials. There is also an informative guidebook on the purposes and functions of the Fed in the "About the Fed" section of the web site. At the web site for the Federal Reserve Bank of New York, www.ny.frb.org, you can find a history of the changes Fed policy makers have made in their short-term interest rate benchmark, the federal funds rate, which they use to implement their monetary policy.

As for what the new chairman of the Fed, Ben S. Bernanke, is going to tell investors, we think he may turn out to be a little different from his predecessor, Alan Greenspan. Bernanke seems to be more interested in telling investors what the Fed is thinking, rather than what the Fed is going to do, which became Greenspan's specialty. If this is the case, then watching key economic indicators, like data on employment and inflation, is going to be important for investors. Combined with what Bernanke says about the Fed's current thinking, this kind of economic data will become the better indicator of what the Fed is going to do next.

Of course there are plenty of newspaper and magazine stories and television commentaries on what the Fed is doing and going to do. And any investor can go to the PIMCO web site, at www.pimco.com/TopNav/Home, to find out what Paul McCulley's current thinking is on the Fed.

As for figuring out what the market thinks about the Fed, one way is to look at the futures contracts for the federal funds rate, which is the overnight rate on loans between banks. These monthly contracts give an indication of what investors think the

Fed will be doing with the fed funds rate over the next several months.

Based on work by some economists at the Federal Reserve and elsewhere, these futures contracts are not precise indicators at all. One study even has contended that they are not even very good indicators of investor sentiment because many investors are drawn to buy them not to bet on what the Fed policy makers will be doing in the future but just for the possible profit.[1]

But these futures contracts can give investors a sense of what many think is the direction and speed of rate increases or decreases, as well as a signal that a Fed that has been on hold is about to change its policy. In addition, if there is some surprising news, such as a much stronger or weaker than expected employment report, the response of the fed funds futures contracts can indicate to investors how much this new economic report is changing opinions on the outlook for Fed policy.

Fed funds futures contracts can be seen on the web site of the Chicago Board of Trade, at www.cbot.com, by clicking on 30-day fed funds. (As of the end of 2006, the CBOT was planning to merge with the Chicago Mercantile Exchange.) What you see on this page of the CBOT site is the fed funds futures contracts by month and their prices. Subtracting the price from 100 gives you the approximate level of the average fed funds rate that is predicted for that month. There is more detail on fed funds futures and how to read them at the web site of the Federal Reserve Bank of Cleveland, at www.clevelandfed.org/research/policy/fedfunds/faq.cfm.

Now, of course, with all of this information available, it is not that hard to know that the Fed has changed its policy, or even that a change in policy is approaching. The advantage of the PMI and fed funds futures is that, combined, they can give an investor a small jump. Stocks and bonds don't wait for the Fed, but rather take their cue from the PMI. So maybe you, too, can move some money around a little ahead of time and pick up some more risk for your portfolio as you do it.

DEFINING THE FED

Job. The central bank has a mandate to promote maximum employment, stable prices, and moderate long-term interest rates. It has often gotten caught in the conflict between the demands for more jobs and lower inflation.

But after the crippling double-digit inflation of the 1970s, the public and the politicians seemed to accept the fact that the Fed has the right to be preemptive and tighten its reins on the economy, curb the growth of jobs, and flirt with a recession, even if there are no obvious signs of a nasty acceleration in inflation. This kind of preemptive tightening was the way the Fed brought down the inflation rate over the past three decades, and it seems that voters and politicians alike are willing to take the pain in exchange for the benefits of an economy with stable prices.

In the conflict between jobs and inflation, the central bank favors beating inflation, in part because policy makers believe that is the core job of a central bank. But it is also easier for the Fed to lean against jobs if it has to because its goal of sustainable economic growth is not defined. Instead, it is what Fed policy makers say it is, and of course, that makes it a moving target. While inflation also is not officially defined, it has come over time to be seen as under control when it is at 2 percent or less, using a price barometer that excludes volatile food and energy prices. (See Core PCE.)

Who Decides. There are 12 voting members of the Federal Open Market Committee (FOMC). The seven governors of the Federal Reserve Board and the president of the Federal Reserve Bank of New York, which is the place where the Fed's interest rate decisions are put into effect, always vote. The four other votes are rotated among the other 11 Federal Reserve bank presidents. These four Federal Reserve bank presidents serve one-year terms on a rotating basis, but all the bank presidents can attend and argue at the FOMC meetings.

(Continued)

DEFINING THE FED *(Continued)*

The FOMC meets about every six weeks, or eight times a year, at the Federal Reserve's headquarters in Washington, D.C. There are six one-day meetings and two meetings of two days each. The two-day meetings come at the beginning and middle of the year and are followed by the chairman's semiannual report to Congress on monetary policy, in which the FOMC sets out a detailed assessment of the economic outlook. The FOMC can also meet by telephone and make policy changes in between regular meetings, if members think a change is necessary.

After every meeting, the FOMC issues a statement in which the action taken is explained, even if the federal funds target is left unchanged. The language of these statements and how it is altered from meeting to meeting is what Fed watchers feast on.

But despite the voting, the FOMC is not as democratic as it may appear. The Fed needs strong leadership because dissension among these policy makers over whether to raise or lower interest rates would be unsettling for financial markets, as investors try to guess which faction might win in the long run. So the chairman, in recent history, has been the first among equals.

Alan Blinder, a governor of the Fed from June 1994 to January 1996, said that under Alan Greenspan, the Federal Open Market Committee was an "autocratically collegial committee," in which the chairman set the consensus of the group. The chairman, Blinder said, "may begin the meeting with the decision already made and simply inform the other members. Or he may listen to the debate and then announce the group's consensus, expecting everyone else to fall in line. But in either case, the group's decision is essentially the chairman's decision, hopefully informed by, and perhaps even influenced by, the views of the other committee members."[2]

Tools. The Fed has a system or mechanism for implementing its monetary policy, but it has had to be redesigned several times because it has failed to work as promised. For example, the system of the 1970s was tossed into the dustbin, according to the Fed guidebook, because it did "not have great success in combating the increase in inflationary pressures that resulted from oil-price shocks and excessive money growth over the decade."[3] The Fed has had four steering regimes since the 1970s.

Federal Funds Target. The current steering mechanism is the target policy makers set for the overnight interest rate for loans between banks, known as the federal funds rate, or fed funds rate. This rate is raised or lowered when Fed policy makers are trying to adjust the mix of growth and inflation in the economy—up when there is too much inflation and Fed policy makers want to restrict credit and growth and down when there is too little growth and policy makers want to loosen their reins on credit to encourage economic growth.

Tightening. When the Fed is raising its target for the federal funds rate.

Easing. When the Fed is lowering its target for the federal funds rate.

Open Market Operations. The purchase or sale of securities by the Federal Reserve and the mechanism by which the Fed moves the actual federal funds rate up or down to meet the target it has set for its policy. These purchases and sales control the reserve balances that banks are required to hold against their checking account deposits. The reserves are just a fraction of the total deposits. When the Federal Reserve, through the Federal Reserve Bank of New York, buys securities, it is adding to the level of reserves. When the Fed sells securities it is reducing the level of reserves. When the Fed changes the supply of reserves relative to banks' demand, the price of reserves—the

(Continued)

DEFINING THE FED *(Continued)*

federal funds rate—rises or falls, stimulating or restraining the public's demand for credit. Policy makers try to keep the actual fed funds rate as close as possible to the target rate, but there are times when these rates can be far apart, for seasonal reasons and other temporary distortions.

Discount Window. This is the Fed's safety valve. Through the discount window the Fed can act as the lender of last resort when the financial markets are disrupted, whether it be by a financial mishap or a terrorist attack. On September 11, 2001, the day of the terrorist attacks, the Fed issued a press release saying: "The Federal Reserve System is open and operating. The discount window is available to meet liquidity needs."[4] The discount window can also make loans to individual banks that are under financial stress. In the course of regular open market operations, loans through the discount window can also relieve upward pressure on the fed funds rate.

Phillips Curve. The Phillips curve is a measure of the relationship between inflation and unemployment and has come to mean that when inflation is high, unemployment is low, and vice versa. So when unemployment gets "too" low, a jump in inflation is expected.

Most economists—and certainly most Fed policy makers—argue that in the long run there is no trade-off between unemployment and inflation. If this is true, the Fed cannot permanently buy lower unemployment with a higher inflation rate, and attempts to do so will result only in higher inflation. So modern-day monetary orthodoxy holds that in the long run, the Fed's mission to promote growth and stable prices collapses to a single mission: fighting inflation.

But this argument avoids dealing with the short-term cost of inflation fighting, which is throwing people out of work. Karl Marx called these conscripted citizens in the fight against inflation the reserve army of the unemployed.

In recent years, the Phillips curve trade-off between unemployment and inflation has been weakening in the United States, which means that a drop in unemployment should produce less upward pressure on wages than in the past. This is because labor costs embedded in the products and services we consume are now a function of global wages—which are lower—as well as U.S. wages.

This is hugely important for Fed policy. Now that U.S. labor's power to demand higher wages is diminished by competition from a global labor supply, the Fed need not worry that a falling U.S. unemployment rate will quickly generate a rapid acceleration in U.S. wage-driven inflation.

NAIRU. The nonaccelerating inflation rate of unemployment (NAIRU) is the level at which the unemployment rate is the lowest it can be without causing an acceleration in inflation. This concept is anathema to those who dismiss the validity of a cyclical Phillips curve, especially after the stagflation of the 1970s showed that inflation and unemployment could rise at the same time. But in reality, NAIRU remains at the core of the Fed's reaction function. So when the unemployment rate begins to rise, Fed policy makers really take notice.

Taylor Rule. The Taylor rule is a formula that can give one an idea of what the neutral federal funds rate is. At neutral, the fed funds rate is believed to be neither stimulating nor impeding economic growth, and, therefore, it is the place where policy makers are often likely to stop a tightening or easing cycle. The Taylor rule can also be used to figure out how much the Fed has to raise interest rates to get inflation back to a stable level or to cut interest rates to get economic growth up to its sustainable level. Fed policy makers, however, are unlikely to ever make either of these calculations in public. Instead, they say they will know when the fed funds rate is at the right level when they see it, similar to the Supreme Court's doctrine in the matter of defining pornography.

(Continued)

DEFINING THE FED *(Continued)*

Core PCE. The deflator for personal consumption expenditures, excluding volatile food and energy costs, the core PCE is the inflation barometer that Fed policy makers follow most closely. It is based on the data collected by the government to calculate the gross domestic product, which is the measure of the economy's output of goods and services, and its real—or inflation-adjusted—growth rate. Fed officials worry about the inflation rate excluding food and energy because food and energy prices can be volatile, distorting what Fed policy makers call the underlying rate of inflation.

For example, the PCE, excluding food and energy prices, was 2.2 percent for the 12 months through November 2006 and 2.3 percent for the 12 months through June 2006. But the PCE, including food and energy prices, was 1.9 percent for the 12 months through November 2006, down from 3.5 percent in June, because of a drop in the price of oil. Fed policy makers do not want to have their policy moved by such volatility. They get worried only if these swings in the price of food and energy begin to lift the underlying rate of inflation. So when Fed officials talk about the inflation rate being worrisome, they are talking about the rate of inflation excluding food and energy prices—the underlying rate.

Transparency. The Fed is probably now the most open closed institution in Washington, D.C. It has come a long way from the years when Fed watchers had to examine reams of Fed data just to guess whether policy makers had made a change in their monetary policy stance. Now Fed policy is announced, as is the central bank's near-term intention for interest rates. In forecasting the future policy, Fed policy makers have gone as far as guaranteeing in writing that interest rates would remain low for a long time, or, as they put it, "a considerable period."

Greenspan Put. This refers to the putative promise to ease quickly and aggressively if stock prices crash, while, at the same time, being usually unwilling to lean against stock prices when they are rising rapidly. It is a promise that many in the financial markets believe that Greenspan made. It has contributed to the willingness of investors to take on more risk because of their belief that the Fed will be there to bail them out if the stock market goes sour. This feeling of being protected increases what is called moral hazard, which reduces the incentive to pay attention to risks.

Intervention. Another key job of the Fed is to intervene in the foreign exchange markets, if necessary, to strengthen or weaken the dollar. Such interventions are done in conjunction with the U.S. Treasury, with the Federal Reserve Bank of New York doing the buying or selling of dollars as the agent for the FOMC and the Treasury. Such currency interventions do not happen often; the Fed has intervened in the foreign exchange market only a few times since 1995.

The most famous interventions, which included the Fed and other major central banks around the world, were during the global effort to weaken the dollar after the Plaza Accord in September 1985 and the following effort to strengthen the dollar after the Louvre Accord in February 1987.

Fed Watchers. These are analysts who scrutinize every action the Fed takes and every word policy makers utter, all in an attempt to tell investors what the central bank will be doing next and in a few months from then. The job of the Fed watcher is very similar to that of the theologian: identifying the dogmas and catechisms of the secular god of money creation, and within that paradigm of understanding, forecasting feasts and famines for stocks and bonds.

Despite the transparency of the Fed, you cannot depend on the Fed watchers of Wall Street—even McCulley—to get it right all the time. Fed watchers get tripped up by their own view of what they think Fed policy makers should be doing, rather than just figuring out what the policy makers are likely to do. In addition, if policy makers are having trouble with their billiards bank shots, the Fed watchers will have trouble figuring where the cue ball is going next.

THE FED'S CUE BALL

Saying what the Fed does is simple: It uses the powers it has to stabilize prices while allowing the economy to grow without causing inflation. Doing this is very difficult, though, because there is no simple connection between the Fed's operating lever—the raising or lowering of the fed funds rate—and the pace of growth or inflation. An intelligent policy can fail to get the results policy makers expected. Because of this, policy may take a turn that the FOMC was not expecting and that FOMC members never talked about when they were airing their thoughts in public. To describe the degrees of difficulty in what the Fed does we will use billiards and a bowling ball.

Imagine a game of billiards with rules requiring that you call the ball that you plan to pocket, but prohibiting you from striking that ball directly: Your cue ball must first hit either one rail or another ball that has not been called. Think about how you would play this game. Once you've figured it out, you will be qualified to be a central banker.

This is precisely the game played by the members of the FOMC. Their current cue ball is the federal funds rate on overnight loans between banks, which they control.

But policy makers cannot aim their cue ball—the fed funds rate—directly at their ultimate goals of price stability and maximum employment. Rather, they must aim their cue ball at some intermediate variable—the cushion or another ball—which has a predictable impact on price stability and maximum employment—in other words, a bank or another ball with a history of deflecting the cue ball to where the Fed policy makers want it to go.

The problem here is not just that the shot itself is difficult. In addition, the history of the reaction of the cue ball to the cushion or another ball shows that one cannot rely on a particular deflection. Take, for example, the monetary aggregates—or money supply—which include currency, checking accounts, savings deposits, money-market accounts, small certificates of deposit, and money-market mutual funds. Once upon a time, the monetary aggregates were thought to be the cushion or other ball that the cue ball could be aimed at because there was a relationship between them and the growth of the nominal gross domestic product, which includes both real growth and inflation. In other words, the monetary aggregates would deflect the cue ball to the right place. Indeed, the Humphrey-Hawkins Act of 1978 explicitly required the Fed to establish and announce targets for the monetary aggregates.

But this deflecting relationship has proved faulty because of what is called velocity, which is the rate of turnover of the stock of money, or how much it is reused. If velocity is high, for example, the money supply can be smaller and still meet the same goal on growth and inflation. But if velocity speeds up suddenly, then the desired size of the money supply could allow for too much growth and too much inflation.

Without reliable bank shots, Fed policy makers have to hope that their changes in the level of the fed funds rate will be deflected to an array of asset prices—most directly, short-term interest rates, and less directly, longer-term interest rates. The difficulty of these bank shots can be reduced some by what policy makers say in official statements, testimony, and other comments about the trajectory of the fed funds rate in the future.

The move in interest rates in response to the change in the fed funds target and its projected future path affects decisions across the economy, from the borrowing by businesses to build new plants to the decisions by homeowners to refinance their mortgages, which could produce thousands of extra dollars for them to spend. The stock market can also be influenced by these changes in interest rates and, in turn, can affect the decisions of both businessmen and consumers and, therefore, the pace of economic growth or the rate of inflation.

It is often said, especially by members of the Federal Reserve, that policy makers really do not target asset prices in their billiards game, only the real economy. But that is like saying a physician does not target your cholesterol level, just the good health of your heart.

Doctors cannot get directly at their patients' hearts, whereas they can—or at least try to—get directly at their diets by cutting out the high-cholesterol macaroni and cheese.

And the Fed operates in the same fashion regarding the economy's health, using both deed and word regarding the fed funds rate to influence the economy's diet.

But this makes the Fed's job sound too simple, because while policy makers can change the diet, they cannot say exactly how it will affect the patient—the economy—or how quickly.

THE FED'S BOWLING BALL

A house ball, like the ones rented at your local lanes, is drilled for the fingers to grip to the second knuckle. A fancy bowling ball, with a fingertip grip, is drilled shallow, with room for only the tips of the fingers, not quite to the first knuckle. It is an absolute joy to roll. The tricky thing, however, is to actually let it roll.

In contrast to the house ball, configured with the objective of a straight roll into the pocket between the head pin and the one next to it, a fingertip ball is designed to hook, sweeping into the pocket with a lot of spinning action, generating an explosive conflagration among the pins, known as action. There's nothing like it when it works. But you have to let the ball do the work and avoid overpowering its natural hook proclivity.

Simply put, you have to resist both too much speed and letting the wrist rotate in a twisting fashion. With too much speed, the ball will roll through the break, sliding off to the right of the head pin; and with too much wrist action, the ball will overhook, missing the head pin way to the left. The right way to throw a fingertip ball is to resist accelerating the arm on the downswing, while letting it roll gently off the fingers at release.

Fed policy makers use a fingertip ball, and they must not only get their speed and wrist action right but also adjust for the conditions of the lanes. Lanes are regularly oiled, but not necessarily with a regular quantity. Sometimes the lane keeper applies a lot and sometimes a little, and sometimes both at the same time, which is the worst.

Such vagaries in oil application do not really matter when throwing a straight ball. But when rolling a fingertip ball, lane conditions matter a lot because they influence the timing and the vigor of the ball's natural hooking trajectory.

Financial conditions—the animal spirits of the financial market—are the lane conditions for Fed policy makers. Often, like fingertip bowlers, policy makers do not know how lane conditions will change the path, speed, and spin of a perfectly thrown fingertip ball. They can hike the fed funds rate or they can cut the fed funds rate, but if there is an unexpected change in financial conditions—such as a shift in the risk appetite of investors—the change in the fed funds rate will not do what they want it to do.

So, even if you got the rhythm of rolling the ball down perfectly, you still have to make allowances for lane conditions, frequently shifting your feet a board or two to the left or right of neutral on your approach.

That is how tricky central banking is today. One board too far can spell trouble in a world where policy makers not only have to worry about inflation, but also have to ward off any deflationary threat and figure out how the constant evolution of the financial system, like the oil on a bowling alley, affects the roll of their monetary policy ball.

How wrong can things go? Well, there are plenty of times when things did not work the way policy makers intended.

In 1994, even if Fed policy makers thought that investors, traders, money managers, and analysts should have known about the increase in interest rates that was coming, the markets were not prepared. And the announcement of a quarter of a percentage point rate hike on February 4, 1994, and the seven rate increases that followed triggered a sell-off in the bond market that produced the worst year since the inception of the Lehman Brothers U.S. Aggregate Index in 1976, with a 2.9 percent loss. Stocks were flat for the year, with the Standard & Poor's 500 stock index down 1.5 percent in price and up only 1.3 percent with dividends.

In this case, Fed policy makers got a much worse market performance than they had bargained for.

In the 2004 to 2006 cycle of rate increases, the bond market seemed to ignore the sharp rise in short-term interest rates for almost the entire period, as the appetite for risk was much heartier than anticipated. For this reason, longer-term interest rates did not rise as would have been expected and Fed policy makers had to raise the short-term interest rate target higher than even some policy makers may have expected.

The lane conditions of 2004 to 2006 are likely to be the same in the future if the bond market continues to believe that the Fed has a lot of anti-inflation credibility and policy makers are attempting a gradual tightening.

One reason for this is that the bond market, under current conditions, does not worry about inflation in the future, only about how much the Fed has to raise interest rates to restrain it. There is no fear that inflation will get out of hand or that the Fed, in an oft-used phase of years ago, will get behind the curve. So it is not inflation that is pushing interest rates higher, just the anticipation of interest rates going higher to curb inflation. So inflation scares are really not inflation scares anymore. They are just interest rate scares in drag.

HISTORY OF THE GAME

The central bank game, whether it is metaphorically closer to billiards or to bowling now, has been evolving over the past three decades.

Prior to the 1980s, central banking, as an operation, was child's play, even if the policy makers did not perform that well. Monetary policy worked its magic through a highly regulated, essentially closed domestic financial system centered on commercial banks and thrifts and savings banks. Regulation Q capped the interest rate that commercial banks could pay on deposits at one-quarter of a percentage point below what thrifts and savings banks could pay. In return for that quarter-point advantage in attracting deposits, thrifts were required to deploy the lion's share of their deposits into long-term, fixed-rate home mortgages.

It was ideal for the Fed, because it gave policy makers colossal power over the availability and pricing of credit, which is the fuel for growth. If the economy was overheating and inflation was a threat, policy makers could easily tighten the screws on the nation's housing market because of Regulation Q.

All policy makers had to do was raise short-term interest rates above the deposit rate ceiling that thrifts could pay. This would drain money out of thrifts as investors moved their money to Treasury securities paying higher yields. And quickly the fuel for the housing market—credit through mortgages—was gone. There was a credit crunch, with thrifts literally having no new money to lend out for mortgages. In that world, housing credit was rationed by the availability of cash at the thrifts, not, as it is today, with onerous mortgage interest rates.

But double-digit inflation brought an end to Regulation Q, as the rate of price increases rose above the ceiling on the deposit rates at banks and thrifts and inspired the kind of financial entrepreneurship that has been going on ever since. In this case, it was the advent of money-market funds, which did not have limits on the interest they could pay on deposits. In addition, this period gave birth to the so-called securitization of mortgages, which meant thrifts no longer had to keep them on their books. Instead, they were sold to other investors in the secondary market.

It was a move that was great for homeowners because it made more mortgage money available. But it also changed the way credit was allocated, basically taking it out of the hands of the banks—and, therefore, further away from the control of Fed policy makers. Credit was no longer rationed according to the availability of deposits in banks. It became as easy to buy as a bushel of soybeans at whatever price—interest rate—the market would bear.

Paul A. Volcker, who began the Fed's successful fight against inflation in 1979, became chairman as these changes were occurring. He was immediately faced with two problems. The first was to figure out a better way to implement the central bank's monetary policy. The second was to invent a way to keep the Fed from being blamed for the astronomically high interest rates that would be needed to begin to break the back of the double-digit inflation that was then rampant.

Volcker achieved both of these goals when he announced, on October 6, 1979, that he was switching the Fed's instrument of policy from one that adjusted the federal funds rate on overnight loans between banks (yes, that is the instrument of policy that is being used today) to one that made growth in nonborrowed reserves the instrument of policy.

Reserves were the required balances that banks held against their deposits, and by targeting the level of one component of these reserves, the Fed would be able to control the growth of the money supply. If the money supply grew too fast, which would mean too much economic growth and more inflation, banks would have to increase their reserves. And to do that they would have to borrow in the federal funds market, pushing up the fed funds rate. Nonborrowed reserves were reserves that had not been borrowed by banks through the Federal Reserve's discount window.

The Fed, in its guidebook, notes, with a bit of understatement, how this new instrument of policy forced banks to bid up the fed funds rates, "sometimes sharply."[5]

In this new world, the fed funds rate would be market-determined. The Fed was not driving up interest rates; the Fed was just prudently restraining growth in the money stock. It was all a ruse, of course, to induce a recession—the only proven path to breaking an insidious spiral of rising inflation and even faster-rising inflationary expectations. But as a practical matter, this change in operations by Volcker meant that policy makers could let the fed funds rate rise to 20 percent while claiming, "Look, Ma, no hands!" During this period the yield on the Treasury's 30-year bond, which was then the benchmark Treasury security, breeched 15 percent.

The Fed's game changed again in 1982, as Volcker was bringing down the sky-high fed funds rate quickly and the link between the money supply and the pace of growth and inflation was breaking down. Fed policy makers moved to using borrowed reserves, which were lent through the discount window, as their instrument of policy and Volcker blew smoke about how the Fed's money growth targets were being distorted by financial deregulation.

But Fed policy was still well disguised, because the policy makers did not go back to targeting the fed funds rate directly. Instead, they began to target what they called "the degree of pressure on reserve positions," which was influenced by the limiting or easing of the Fed's control of borrowed reserves. It was a lot of misdirection that best served the community of Fed watchers because it gave them a lot to do and made it seem like they were doing a lot.

Finally, after the crash of 1987, the Fed gave up on indirectly targeting the fed funds rate via a discount window borrowings target. The Fed had to go back to directly pegging the fed funds rate and had to acknowledge that was what it was doing. But Fed watchers still had jobs, because the Fed didn't announce when it changed its fed funds peg; Fed watchers still had to look for signs of policy changes wherever they could find them.

But that all began to change in February of 1994, when the Fed said that it was starting a new tightening campaign and, for the first time, announced the decision publicly right after it was made. In July 1995, the Fed began to make its target for the fed funds rate public in the announcements after an FOMC meeting.

This was a regime change in communications, and with that Fed watching died as a plumber's job and became an economist's job. Before these changes, Fed watchers, even if they were economists, were really plumbers because their job was to understand the flow of reserves of various descriptions through the Federal Reserve system and what that meant for the money supply, interest rates, and, then, the economy. And with this plumbing expertise they were also called on to announce when Fed policy makers had changed policy, because the Fed did not tell anyone. Now Fed watchers have returned their focus to the real economy and have to be masters of high-frequency responses to the release of monthly and quarterly economic data, which is where they now look for signs of a coming change in Fed policy.

FED MOMENTS

The financial panics at the end of the 1800s and the beginning of the 1900s were the main impetus behind the creation of the Federal Reserve. A central bank was needed to become the lender of last resort in a banking crisis, replacing a system of individual banks and associations, all of whom tried to protect themselves against runs.

Another rationale was that money is too dangerous to be left to popularly elected politicians, who would naturally be tempted to use the printing press to cover the gap between politically inspired promises (to spend more or to tax less) and the ability of the economy to deliver in a noninflationary way.

When the Federal Reserve and its 12 regional banks were established in 1913, the first goal, a central bank that could act as a lender of last resort, was achieved, even if Fed policy makers failed in this role during the Depression. But it was not until 1951 that the Federal Reserve finally secured its independence, as much as is possible, from politics.

This independence, which gave the nation's central bankers operational freedom on monetary policy, came with an accord between the Fed and the U.S. Treasury that said the central bank no longer would be committed to keeping interest rates low on government bonds.

The Fed had agreed to such an interest rate peg during World War II to reduce the costs of government borrowing to pay for the war, and had continued it after 1945. But in 1950, as war began in Korea, inflation pressures were rising and Fed policy makers wanted to raise interest rates. The Treasury of President Truman did not and, at the time, the Treasury was calling the shots.

The confrontation that followed was bitter at times, and after it was over the then chairman of the Federal Reserve, Thomas B. McCabe, was forced to resign. But inflationary pressures, the need to fight them, and support in Congress and the press helped the Fed prevail. The interest rate peg was dropped, and Fed policy makers had to relearn how to manage growth and inflation.[6] The Fed cemented that independence when it successfully won the war against inflation half a century later.

With this independence, the Fed becomes the referee between the competing needs of democracy and capitalism.

Democracy inherently favors soft money or, if you prefer, populist money. This is because soft money lubricates the ability of our leaders to promise the electorate more in goodies than we are collectively willing to fund via taxes. In addition, soft money, through unanticipated inflation, redistributes income and wealth from creditors to debtors, the latter outnumbering the former.

In contrast, capitalism inherently favors hard money or, if you prefer, honest money. This is because hard money serves as a straitjacket to keep democratically elected fiscal authorities honest, preventing them from trying to redistribute a bigger economic pie than Adam Smith's invisible hand can create in a noninflationary way. In addition, hard money protects the real value of the wealth of creditors, who are outnumbered by debtors at the ballot box.

The Fed's mission is to straddle the competing interests of soft and hard money advocates. The democratically elected legislature's job is to hold the Fed accountable for the trade-offs it makes between the competing interests of debtors and creditors.

Nowadays, legislators genuflect to central bank authorities, acting as if the Congress reports to the Federal Reserve, not the other way around. This was especially the case with Greenspan, whose every utterance on monetary policy was taken as gospel, while legislators groveled for his endorsement of their fiscal and regulatory proposals.

Fiscal policy is the last bastion of democratically driven policy in this country and, therefore, it is distressing that the fiscal policy makers—the Congress and the president—feel they need to seek the Fed chairman's blessing for their fiscal policy preferences. This is especially true now that the country has reached the promised land of "effective price stability."

During the war against inflation, a strong argument could be made that it was imperative that the monetary authority dominate the fiscal authority. Simply put, if the monetary authority was going to be systematically leaning on the aggregate demand brake, as required to successfully bring down inflation, it would be counterproductive for the fiscal policy of the president and the Congress to be simultaneously leaning on the aggregate demand accelerator.

And not only was this the case economically, it was also the case in the context of democracy: We the people had said that we wanted inflation vanquished. Thus, it made both economic and democratic sense for the Fed to browbeat fiscal authorities to tighten up. Volcker successfully browbeat President Reagan in 1984, forcing him, with the threat of still tighter money policy, to hike taxes as part of a midcourse fiscal policy correction. Greenspan did the same to the first President Bush, forcing him, by refusing to ease aggressively in the recession, to eat his "read my lips" pledge to not raise taxes and to actually raise them. And he also did it to President Clinton, seducing him, with the promise of continued easy money, into recanting on his pledge to cut taxes for the middle class.

Whether you agreed or disagreed with those Fed-inspired tax hikes, the rationale was simple, both economically and democratically. But that condition no longer holds. Inflation is no longer Public Enemy Number One. Thus, the fiscal authority need not bow down to the monetary authority as if the war against inflation were still being fought.

OTHER CENTRAL BANKS

Central banks other than the Fed began to play a greater role in the global economy in the 1990s. One reason was that they were necessary in the fight against inflation in many countries, especially emerging market countries. Another reason is that more of them became independent, the biggest one being the new European Central Bank, now speaking in a single voice for the 12 countries using the euro. And as we have already noted, China's central bank has had a big influence on interest rates, inflation, and the dollar and will continue to in the years ahead.

The oldest central bank is Sweden's Riksbank, which was begun in 1668, followed by the Bank of England in 1694. In all there are more than 100 central banks and they are becoming more independent all the time. One of the more important central banks to gain its independence recently was the Bank of Japan, which was freed from the grip of Japan's Ministry of Finance in 1998.

While the central banks in the world's developed countries are similar in function to the Federal Reserve, their styles can be very different. One issue is whether a central bank has an expressed inflation target. The Fed, as we have noted, does not. The European Central Bank does. It is 2 percent.

Another style difference is whether a central bank will use its target short-term interest rate solely to influence growth in aggregate demand for goods and services relative to aggregate supply, or will it also use it to preempt or prick asset price bubbles?

The Fed says no, as we have noted, while both the European Central Bank and the Bank of Japan say yes. This difference is key to understanding—and forecasting—the relative monetary policy among the three institutions and, thus, the prospective course for the exchange rates of the dollar, the euro, and the yen. What it means is that the dollar is likely to be weaker than it otherwise would be over the longer term against the euro and the yen, as the Fed, eschewing preemptive bubble popping, is forced to push short-term interest rates lower than their counterparts to prompt a recovery during postbubble periods. So there could be more to be made by Americans if they shift portions of their portfolios abroad.

One more way to see how the rest of the world's central banks are making a difference for American, and other, investors is to look at the surprising behavior of longer-term interest rates while the Federal Reserve was raising its fed funds target by 4.25 percentage points from June 2004 to August 2006.

One reason that longer-interest rates remained unusually low was that two other major central banks, in addition to the Federal Reserve, took actions that were in their own interests and, at the same time, helped reduce the risk level in global markets. And that made for lower longer-term interest rates, as investors who saw the risk level decline bought more, pushing up the prices of bonds and bringing down interest rates. Stock prices also benefited in the lower-risk environment, which took three central banks to create—a sort of de facto monetary union.

Since 1995, the People's Bank of China, as explained in Chapter 3, had pegged China's currency, the yuan, to the dollar, which reduced the risk of dollar depreciation.

Starting in February 2001, the Bank of Japan committed itself to absorbing Japanese short-term interest rate risk via its zero interest rate policy (ZIRP), reinforced by its quantitative easing (QE) policy. Despite the off-putting policy titles, what Japan's central bank was doing was similar to what the Federal Reserve did during and after World War II, before it gained its independence from the Treasury: It guaranteed to keep interest rates low—near zero—to try to restart economic growth and get prices rising to beat deflation.

At the Federal Reserve, policy makers decided to remove their very accommodative policy of low interest rates at a measured pace, with well-telegraphed rate increases of a just a quarter of a percentage point each time the FOMC met.

Each central bank rationally entered into its commitment for sound domestic reasons. In China's case, the rationale was to import a nominal anchor for its own monetary policy, consistent with its mercantilist growth strategy. By pegging the yuan to the dollar, China effectively tied itself to the Fed's monetary policy. In Japan's case, the rationale was to reflate from the deflationary swamp. And in the case of the United States, the rationale was to cut off the risk of deflation at the pass.

In all three cases, the central banks were acting as insurance agents, underwriting risks that the global markets would otherwise have had to absorb and price. Such market pricing would have meant higher interest rates, lower stock prices, and slower economic growth.

The risk protection provided by the three central banks is called moral hazard. Reducing the risk—or hazard—in markets makes investors willing to make more bets. Its good feeling is similar to that of deposit insurance, which frees depositors from having to absorb and price the risk of their banks going belly-up or to have to sit up nights worrying about it. More important, moral hazard means that investors will be less wary.

To be sure, these actions by the three central banks were not as explicit or as robust as deposit insurance. But they were explicitly cut from the same bolt of moral hazard cloth in all three cases as intended inducements to more risk-seeking behavior by the private sector. Why? Because as animal spirits rise so does the potential for economic growth, and that creates an environment that is not conducive to deflation.

It was fun, as always is the case in the beginning of moral hazard–driven schemes, as lower risk premiums were turned into profits as global markets rode on the wings of the big three central banks' commitments to absorb volatility risks.

The debate as to whether the big three should have done what they did frequently takes on a religious character. But regardless of your persuasion in these matters, there should be no doubt about what occurred: a concerted global effort of reflation among leading central banks—that is, a monetary policy that would do its best to guarantee that prices and inflation would begin to rise. The problem with such an antideflation policy is the risk that the result will be more inflation than anyone wanted.

5

Prices and the Fed

You might ask, why is Chapter 5 not called "Inflation and the Federal Reserve"? The answer is that inflation is not a threat in the current environment—or over the next three to five years. Disinflation, which means the pace of price increases is slowing down, and deflation, which means prices are actually falling, are. So this chapter is about prices, no matter what direction they are moving in.

The Fed, of course, is the other half of the title because its 7 governors and 12 regional Federal Reserve bank presidents are the officials who will decide pretty much single-handedly what impact price movements in any direction have on the economy. The question here is not whether the policy makers at the nation's central bank know what problems they will face in the years ahead or that they will move to deal with them. Fed officials earned all the anti-inflation credibility they needed in their successful fight against inflation, and Fed officials responded well to the first deflationary scare of the new era of price stability.

But it would help these policy makers—and investors—if they employed a new tool to help them wrestle with the problem of prices moving in any direction. The tool is an inflation target, a range that sets out what the central bank thinks is the acceptable low level and acceptable high level for the pace of price increases.

In an era of price stability, an official inflation target, or range, that is higher than the prevailing inflation rate would be the way for the central bank to build antideflation credibility, the complement it now needs to its hard-won anti-inflation credibility.

We have mentioned earlier in the book the need for an inflation cushion—that is, a slightly higher allowable rate of inflation—as a weapon against disinflation and deflation. What we want to do in this chapter is explain how a range of acceptable high and acceptable low inflation would help Fed policy makers communicate with the financial markets and, it is hoped, make those markets a little less volatile.

And we will once again argue for the inflation cushion because we do not think that Fed policy makers are ready to accept it, but should.

One of the problems is that many Fed policy makers seem to think that no inflation is better than just a little inflation. This attitude was reflected in the meeting of the Federal Open Market Committee (FOMC), which makes the central bank's decisions on interest rates, in September 2006. According to the minutes of this meeting, there was a lot of concern about core inflation, which excludes food and energy. At the time, based on the most recently available data, core inflation, using the Fed's price monitor, was up 2.4 percent for the 12 months ending in July.

"Many meeting participants emphasized that they continued to be quite concerned about the outlook for inflation," the minutes of the meeting said. "Recent rates of core inflation, if they persisted, were seen as higher than consistent with price stability, and participants underscored the importance of ensuring a moderation in inflation."[1]

The minutes added that "several participants worried that inflation expectations could rise and the Federal Reserve's willingness to carry through on its intention to seek price stability could be called into question if cost and price pressures mounted or even if there was no moderation in core inflation." In the end, one member of the Federal Open Market Committee opposed the committee's decision not to raise its target for the fed funds rate, which was at 5.25 percent, any further.

This is a bias against inflation learned in the war for price stability. But that was the last war.

Fed policy makers now need to educate the markets about the new reality: that policy makers need to allow for a bit more inflation before they put the clamp on the economy, or they will not have the cushion they need against deflation.

THE TARGET

There was no need for an inflation target in the days when the central bank's monetary policy firepower was only aimed at rising prices. In that battle, the Fed operated opportunistically, as it allowed a recession to bring down inflation and then moved during the subsequent recovery to see to it that inflation did not bounce back above the new low level reached during the economic downturn. Under this strategy, the Federal Reserve did not induce recessions to lower inflation, but welcomed them for their disinflationary dividends. It was like losing 10 pounds opportunistically when hit with food poisoning.

Setting an explicit inflation target below the prevailing inflation rate back then would have implied a commitment to hit the target on some definable time horizon, giving Fed policy a bent or a harshness that would have cost millions of new jobs by stifling potential economic growth in the name of beating inflation.

But when it became clear that price stability had been achieved and that the dominant cyclical risk was of unwelcome further disinflation—with the low odds/high consequences risk of outright deflation—the beauty of a public, official definition of secular price stability by means of an inflation target became obvious. This target for acceptable low and high inflation would provide a means for the Fed to communicate two-way price risk—that inflation can be too low as well as too high.

Such an inflation target will help Fed policy makers communicate to the financial markets and investors when they will start and stop cutting interest rates to ward off the possibility of a deflationary spiral and when, as has been the case for decades, they will start and stop raising interest rates against the threat of prices rising at too brisk a pace.

The top end of this inflation target should be higher in this era of low and contained inflation; it should be as high as an annual rate of increase of 3 percent for the deflator for personal consumption expenditures (the PCE deflator, excluding food and energy prices: core PCE). The bottom rate should be 1.5 percent, which provides for a nice level of price stability without being too low.

Three percent is a full percentage point over what Fed policy makers have tolerated in the past. The higher than historically allowable rate of inflation means prices have further to fall before they really get worrisome. In addition, the inflation cushion will bring with it an interest rate cushion, as rates will be a little bit higher if inflation is a little bit higher. This interest rate cushion will give Fed policy makers more room to cut interest rates to stimulate the economy and ward off the threat of deflation in the event that a bursting stock or housing bubble or a sharp recession threatens to bring about the kind of slowdown that could transmute itself into an attack of deflation.

An official inflation target takes a lot of the guessing out of watching the Fed. Investors and analysts do not have to wonder about the inflation tolerances of Fed policy makers and they do not have to wait for policy makers to worry about inflation, disinflation, or deflation publicly.

An official target that tells the financial markets that inflation is too low will truncate deflation risk by getting longer-term interest rates to fall almost on their own when the actual inflation rate gets near this too-low level, as investors anticipate rate cuts from the Fed. These lower rates will stimulate aggregate demand growth, which is the antidote to deflation.

An official target would also make the market expect short-term rates to remain low as long as the rate of inflation stayed near the too-low level. And the range of acceptable inflation rates would give the Fed an up-front and credible exit plan from such a commitment to lower interest rates when the deflation risk had been scotched. The movement of the rate of inflation to comfortably above the too-low rate and near the too-high rate would be the signal that the threat of deflation was over and that interest rates would be moving higher again.

For investors the existence of an inflation target could help ward off one downside of a less clear policy guideline: the market sell-off that could follow if investors think inflation is getting out of control, when, in effect, Fed policy makers are working on their cushion against deflation and letting prices get just a tad higher before they rein them in. In other words, there would be a signal from the central bank that it still will be there to curb inflation.

The lack of this kind of inflation target, which would have provided a clearer guide to the Fed's intentions, was in part responsible for the market confusion and resulting wild market swings in interest rates in the spring and summer of 2003.

To be fair, that spring and summer period was the culmination of the Fed's first defense against deflation and it was a learning period for all, Fed policy makers, analysts, and investors. The defense began as Fed policy makers recognized that the bursting of the stock market bubble was a shock to the system that could threaten to bring on deflation. In late 2000, policy makers switched from a policy leaning toward raising interest rates (tightening) to one leaning toward reducing interest rates (easing).

Aggressive easing followed in 2001, with the central bank slashing its short-term interest rate target by 4.75 percentage points to 1.75. But the Fed's fight against deflation was called into question in 2002, when it appeared to the financial markets that there would be no more interest rate cuts. Both banks and the corporate bond market were spooked and froze credit access to companies with lower-level investment-grade credit ratings, a move that threatened to slow economic growth and make the deflationary threat something more than just a threat.

So the central bank responded in both deed and word. On November 6, 2002, policy makers cut their short-term interest rate target by half a percentage point to a stunningly low 1.25 percent and began a full-blown rhetorical campaign about the availability of "unconventional" weapons to attack the deflationary beast—and the Fed's willingness to use them. One of these unconventional weapons would have the Fed step into the Treasury market to buy billions of dollars' worth of 10-year notes, which would force interest rates lower. The focus on this possibility by traders and analysts in the financial markets was sparked, it seems, by a speech in November 2002 by then Fed governor Ben S. Bernanke, in which he made clear how the central bank would not allow deflation to happen.

In the speech, titled "Deflation: Making Sure 'It' Doesn't Happen Here," Bernanke said: "The U.S. government has a technology, called a printing press (or, today, its electronic equivalent), that allows it to produce as many U.S. dollars as it wishes at essentially no cost. By increasing the number of U.S. dollars in circulation, or even by credibly threatening to do so, the U.S. government can also reduce the value of a dollar in terms of goods and services, which is equivalent to raising the prices in dollars of those goods and services. We conclude that, under a paper-money system, a determined government can always generate higher spending and hence positive inflation."[2]

The rumors of unconventional means to bring long-term interest rates lower reached their peak in the spring of 2003. Although that spring and summer did not see actual deflation, concern about deflation risk was running high.

One reason for that came in early May when Fed policy makers officially highlighted the threat of deflation for the first time in the regular statement they issue after a meeting of the Federal Open Market Committee.

For some time, these statements had routinely handicapped the outlook for the central bank's goals of long-run price stability and sustainable economic growth. For example, in January 2003, the statement said the risks were balanced, which meant that it was 50–50 that growth would continue or slow and 50–50 that prices would remain stable or rise.

In the May statement, policy makers said that the risks on growth were "roughly equal," but then added that in contrast, "the probability of an unwelcome substantial fall in inflation, though minor, exceeds that of a pickup in inflation from its already low level."[3] So the threat of deflation was officially on the Fed's table and, therefore, in the market.

Against this background, as seen in Figure 5.1, interest rates did what they should be expected to do: They fell, and quickly, in anticipation that the Fed would move to stave off any deflation threat by reducing interest rates any way it could.

From April 23 to June 13, the yield on the Treasury's 10-year note dropped almost nine-tenths of a percentage point to 3.13

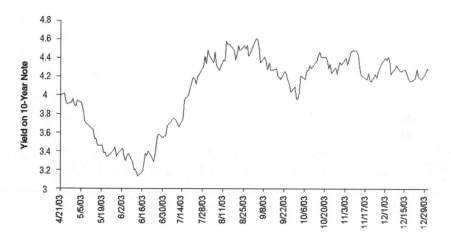

FIGURE 5.1   Volatility Galore

An inflation target might have helped smooth out the wild ride taken by interest rates in 2003.

Source: Federal Reserve.

percent, from 4.02 percent. As other yields fell along with that of the 10-year note, prices rose, and the Treasury market return for those 37 trading days was a stunning 5.4 percent, enough of a return in those eight weeks to match the gain for the 27th best year in the Treasury market since 1973, according to Lehman Brothers. For the month of May alone, the return was 2.9 percent, the 27th best month in the 367 months since 1973.

At the same time, the stock market had begun what turned out to be its first big rally since the bursting of the stock market bubble. (The Standard & Poor's 500 stock index would produce a total return for the year of 28.7 percent.)

The Fed had gotten what it wanted: lower longer-term interest rates that would stimulate economic growth to keep prices and inflation from falling. In fact, policy makers noted the impact of their hint of a deflation threat in their May policy statement during the next meeting of the Federal Open Market Committee in June. And while they did not say so directly, all the results were positive for stimulating growth and defending against the deflation threat.

According to the minutes of that June meeting, policy makers noted that the May policy statement "led market participants to mark down their expectations for the federal funds rate. Consistent with those expectations, Treasury coupon yields declined 35 to 60 basis points [.35 to .60 percentage points]. Yields on corporate bonds also fell about in line with rates on Treasuries even though capital markets absorbed a surge in bond issuance by highly rated firms. Equity prices, buoyed by the decline in bond yields as well as the improved outlook for economic growth, registered sizable gains" between early May and the end of June.[4]

But this antideflation medicine suddenly became toxic—and a nightmare for investors—when Fed policy makers made clear they were not going to give the markets as much help in lowering interest rates as market rumors had anticipated.

While they reduced their target short-term interest rate to 1 percent on June 25, they dashed any hope for an unconventional maneuver to bring longer-term rates even lower. About three weeks after the FOMC meeting, the Fed chairman, Alan Greenspan, told Congress that the central bank would not be stepping into the Treasury market to buy 10-year notes. He did say that the Fed would reduce its target interest rate as low as it could—even to zero, if necessary. But that was not enough, in part because the bond market had already done what it often does: overreacted to rumors of what the Fed might do in the future.

In response, the bond market fell out of bed, as investors and speculators reversed the buying that they had done in anticipation of a big deflation defense, including unconventional moves. It was not a fun July of 2003.

The yield on the 10-year note shot up 1.36 percentage points to 4.49 percent by the end of July and eventually to 4.61 percent at the beginning of September. The loss in the Treasury market for July alone was 4.4 percent. That monthly loss was more than the loss for any entire year in the Treasury market in 30 years.

This Treasury market reversal didn't serve the Fed's antideflation objective at all. So on August 12, the next meeting of the Federal Open Market Committee, policy makers took an unusual step: They said in the statement issued after the meeting that they would keep their short-term interest rate target, already at a record low of 1 percent, at or near that level for "a considerable period."[5]

The minutes of the August FOMC meeting show that policy makers were keenly aware how their decision at the June meeting to reduce their short-term interest rate only by a quarter of a percentage point had disappointed investors, as did squelching the use of any unconventional means to bring interest rates lower. While the stock market did rally, the minutes go on to note how much the yield on 10-year Treasury notes rose and that the yields on investment-grade corporate bonds followed suit.

As for the addition of the pledge to keep interest rates low for "a considerable period," the threat of deflation was at the top of the list of reasons, even though the word *deflation* was never used. Disinflation is a slowdown in price increases, and it was clear to policy makers that a "significant further disinflation" could turn into deflation, the actual decline in prices, according to the minutes of the meeting.[6]

The minutes said that many members of the FOMC saw a "need to encourage progress toward closing the economy's currently wide output gap and, with inflation already near the low end of what some members regarded as an acceptable range, to resist significant further disinflation. In the view of these members, appreciable added disinflation would potentially blunt the effectiveness of further policy easing in the event of strong adverse shocks to the economy. At the same time, maintaining an accommodative policy stance was seen as involving little risk of inducing rising inflation."[7]

Given the market meat grinder investors had just been put through, it took time and reassuring comments from Fed officials to make the central bank's promise something once-burned investors were willing to bet on. But in September, the yield on the 10-year note began to come down, dropping quickly from 4.61 percent to 3.96 percent by October 1 and then bouncing around to finish the year at 4.27 percent.

There is a point to this history. The volatility it describes in the bond market and the steps it details that Fed policy makers had to take to counter that volatility and reach their objectives are both arguments for an inflation target.

The forward-looking commitment to interest rates remaining low that Fed policy makers imparted with the three words "a considerable period" was a brave new step for policy makers, essentially providing a forecast of its policy intentions.

And that is what an inflation target, with a broad enough range, would do on a regular basis. So the question is whether the policy makers, having already moved this far in clarifying their intentions, will now go further. It is clear from the way the Treasury market was roiled in the spring and summer of 2003 that anything the Fed could do to smooth out market responses to its policy would be a good idea.

It does not appear, however, that Fed policy makers are comfortable with a range for an inflation target that is wide enough on the upside of inflation to provide the cushion against deflation that is necessary.

Bernanke, now the chairman of the Fed, favors some kind of inflation target, one he has called the optimal long-term inflation rate (OLIR). And he has support from Frederic S. Mishkin, who joined the Federal Reserve Board in September 2006. But Bernanke has said that he is not advocating either a time frame for hitting the OLIR or, more important, a specific range around the OLIR that would encompass a too-high and too-low inflation rate.

Still, an OLIR is a step in the right direction toward the type of inflation target range that encompasses the risk of both deflation and inflation.

Having the OLIR explicitly on the table would be a step forward in transparency and accountability, by forcing policy makers to clearly communicate policy moves on interest rates against the backdrop of a specific long-term inflation objective. In addition, an OLIR would make the FOMC more rigorous in calculating and testing its views on the sometimes painful trade-off between inflation and employment growth, as is the case in the rigorous inflation reports issued by central banks that have embraced inflation targeting. Sunshine is not only a great disinfectant, but also a great prophylactic against sloppy thinking.

Most important, perhaps, is that this next step in transparency could give central bank policy makers more flexibility—not less—to acknowledge that there needs to be a greater tolerance for a rise in inflation from its currently low and stable level to assure that the central bank can protect the economy from the threat of deflation as well as it has protected the economy from inflation.

Thus, while an OLIR is a good idea, it is not a good idea if the range for the "acceptable" inflation rate is in the 1.5 percent to 2 percent range, which is the Fed's current implicit inflation target. It is stunning that many Fed officials still preach with religious fervor that there is something intrinsically evil about a 2.2 percent inflation rate versus 1.8 percent. Who's kidding whom?

A 1.5 percent to 3 percent range in the core PCE deflator provides for the cushion against deflation that is needed, and sets an appropriate floor for inflation.

Yet because the Fed does not yet have an explicit OLIR, or an explicit and reasonable range of acceptable high and low inflation around it, the financial markets, especially the fixed-income markets, are teased into believing that the central bank must work to keep core inflation at all times in the narrow 1 percent to 2 percent range, or else it will somehow lose long-term credibility as an inflation fighter.

Well, it is time for a change, because the Fed also has to be a fighter of deflation and there is no point in repeating the market turmoil of the spring and summer of 2003.

But if a change does come, we know that there could be an immediate problem—a bad reaction in the financial markets. The announcement of an acceptable inflation range from 1 percent to 3 percent could be a blow to the Fed's anti-inflation credibility.

The Fed simply cannot do this, many will argue, because the FOMC has preached on the 1 percent to 2 percent inflation zone so loudly for so long. But we argue that if the comfort zone is too low, it is too low. And we believe that the Fed could explain that without any loss of anti-inflation credibility.

But because we concede there is a risk the other way, we are content with waiting for a more propitious time for the Fed to formally acknowledge reality. The next easing cycle, which by definition will be about downside risks to growth, not upside risk to inflation, would be an ideal time.

6

McCulley

In this chapter, Paul McCulley is looking in the mirror and you can see what he sees.

We will see McCulley as a money manager, which will give investors insight into how forecasters and mutual funds behave. One of the prime tenets for a bond money manager, McCulley says, is that the fixed-income game is not about winning. It is about not losing.

No, you didn't misread that last sentence. At its core, fixed-income portfolio management is about not losing. Unlike managers of stock portfolios, PIMCO's money managers cannot score ten-baggers. Although it can be painful to take the paper losses, a stock picker can have some aces in the hole and wait for the market to recognize them for what they are. That's a ten-bagger. Fixed-income managers can only pray to get their money back when their securities mature. So, by definition, bond managers play not to lose, while equity managers play to win.

But despite the not-to-lose strategy there is still plenty of money at stake. In just one day, a correct prediction by McCulley that the Fed will unexpectedly raise or lower its fed funds rate by a quarter of a percentage point can mean a $3 billion to $5 billion jump in the value of the $667.7 billion worth of mutual funds and private client funds managed by PIMCO. Good or bad forecasts on important economic data, like the monthly unemployment report, also will move the value of PIMCO's funds up or down by a billion dollars here and a billion dollars there.

After seeing McCulley in the office mirror, we will shift to McCulley's mirror at home and see him as an investor, which will show how important, until recently, his home had been to his net worth and provide a live example of a long-term portfolio, which should, and does, take on extra risk, and a foundation portfolio that is conservative.

A look into a money-manager mirror is not always flattering. But McCulley is as willing to take the blame as he is happy to take the credit, especially if he can tell a good story for investors.

"Even though I was raised as a Baptist, I have a Catholic perspective about confession being good for the soul," he said. "When you have made a mistake you do not find a way to rationalize it. You stand up and say, 'I made a mistake.' You are supposed to be more embarrassed by your mistakes than you are boastful about your successes."

As you have no doubt noticed already, this chapter is completely different in approach from the others in the book because it is *about* McCulley, not written by McCulley. McCulley moves, for this chapter, from the co-author to the third person. We hope that is not jarring, but we thought it was the easiest way to tell this part of the story.

McCULLEY'S BEST BET

On August 7, 2001, Paul McCulley went to the CNBC television studio in Fort Lee, New Jersey, for an interview with Consuelo Mack, who did a daily "Strategy Session" report on the markets and was the anchor and managing editor of the weekly "The *Wall Street Journal* Report."

For all but 14 words, it was a routine three-minute interview, the type that McCulley, and hundreds of other investment talking heads, have done repeatedly. McCulley talked about the sluggish economy, productivity, labor costs—on which new data had just been released—and his preference for bonds over stocks. On his specialty, the Federal Reserve, he said that the central bank would be cutting its benchmark short-term interest rate still further: nothing spectacular.

"I think the Fed has got some more cutting to do. But, more importantly, is once the Fed finishes cutting, I think they have to stay easy for a very, very long period of time," he told Mack. "I think they need to get super low on short rates and stay super low."

But then, all of a sudden, he got bold: "In fact, I think Greenspan has tightened for the last time of his career."

Mack was surprised. "Very interesting," she said. "Okay, we'll hold you to that prediction, Paul."

"Absolutely," McCulley replied, with a quiet chuckle.

How bold was this, to say flatly that the Federal Reserve, under Greenspan's leadership, had raised its benchmark short-term interest rate for the last time? Well, no one was expecting a rate increase anytime soon.

In an effort to avoid a recession after the bursting of the stock market bubble in 2000 left corporate America staggering, the Fed had been cutting its benchmark federal funds rate since that January, reducing it to 3.75 percent from 6.5 percent. The economy was sluggish. The data on the gross domestic product for the second quarter, which was reported late in July, showed that the economy had grown at an annual rate of just 0.7 percent from April through June.

Greenspan had said in testimony to Congress in July that growth could pick up by the end of the year but that he was still worried about the risks that faced the economy. (In fact, a recession, the first in 10 years, had begun in March 2001, five months before McCulley's comment. But the National Bureau of Economic

Research [NBER], the arbiter of the business cycle, did not make that ruling until November 2001. And Greenspan was right, because the recovery began in November 2001, a fact that NBER made official in July 2003.)

What made McCulley's prediction bold was that Greenspan's term on the Fed, at the time, was not up until June of 2004. That meant almost three years without a rate increase. So McCulley had given a specific date that was a long way off. That was a lot different than saying, as he did just before he made this prediction, that he thought the Fed would "have to stay easy for a very, very long period of time." That was an opinion, not a forecast.

In addition, McCulley's prediction came before the 9/11 terrorist attacks, which on their own prompted a series of further Fed rate cuts. And the prediction came well before Fed policy makers began to worry out loud about the threat of deflation, a concern that was not officially voiced until May 2003. Both 9/11 and the threat of deflation became additional reasons for keeping the Fed's target interest rate lower longer, bolstering McCulley's forecast, but after he made it.

McCulley says that the essence of his call was that the bursting of the stock market bubble and the resulting damage to the corporate sector of the economy left the consumer alone to do the work of rekindling economic growth. The way to get the consumer going was to create a housing boom that would give cash back to consumers through home sales and mortgage refinancing. Then they would spend it. But doing this required keeping interest rates very low for a long time, in this case as long as Greenspan was due to be in office.

But McCulley says that while "I had thought about this before the interview, I had not planned to say it on that program." Nor had he discussed his forecast within PIMCO, which meant it also came as a surprise to his colleagues, especially his boss, Bill Gross, the founder and chief investment officer at PIMCO.

In fact, his comment was so unplanned that McCulley had not written about it in his monthly "Fed Focus" column. And even after he made the comment, he did not mention it in any of his subsequent columns until the one for December 2001. (Shortly after his television appearance, however, McCulley did broach the idea with Fuerbringer, who wrote an article in *The New York Times* on August 16, 2001, that included McCulley's prediction.[1])

In the December "Fed Focus" column, "Eight Tracks Don't Fit in a CD Player," McCulley argued that the bond market was wrong to fear that the Fed would begin to raise interest rates in 2002 at the first sign of an economic rebound. (The bond market had sold off on such fears in November of 2001, producing big monthly losses of 1.4 percent in the overall bond market and 2.5 percent in the Treasury market, according to the Lehman Brothers U.S. Aggregate Index.)

McCulley argued that rate increases in 2002 would not fight price increases but threaten deflation because inflation was now in check, a big secular change in the economic environment that he argued was being overlooked. And he said that Greenspan was confident that growing worker productivity could offset any normal inflationary pressures that came with a rebound out of the recession, which by December had been officially declared. So he concluded, in the last line of the column, "Greenspan has tightened for the last time of his career."

But that was the last that was heard of McCulley's prediction, although it turned out that he was right. Greenspan was scheduled, at the time, to leave the Fed in June of 2004—and that was when the Fed began raising its short-term interest rate benchmark again. Yes, Greenspan's term was extended to the end of January 2006 by President George W. Bush, but not until April 2003, long after McCulley's forecast.

McCulley was still relatively new at PIMCO at the time of the prediction. He had joined in April 1999 and had become a partner only in January 2001. He was still feeling his way with Gross. And, as he admits now, he got a lot of grief from some of his colleagues, who were more inclined toward the bond market fear of Fed rate increases as the economy rebounded in 2002. They may not have taken well to McCulley's small jibe at holders of the bond market view in his December "Fed Focus" column.

"With the recession now nine months old and massive Fed easing behind us," he wrote, "the fixed-income market is replaying nightmares of a Fed tightening 'take back.' From a trading perspective, this is understandable: history repeats itself until it doesn't. From an investment perspective, however, anticipating secular change is where the real money is made."

In the end the bond market view—in this case, the conventional view—won out, with fears of Fed tightening in 2002 leading Gross to announce in *Barron's* on March 9, 2002: "It appears that Greenspan may take back the emergency post-9/11 rate cuts."[2] Gross said that by the end of the year, the fed funds rate, which was then 1.75 percent, could be back up to 3 percent.

Gross himself was changing his own view from earlier that year, when he said he did not expect the Fed to raise its short-term interest rate target for the next 12 months to 15 months, a long-term forecast, but nowhere near McCulley's.

McCulley had no warning of this change in Gross's view, although he had seen Gross at PIMCO's Cyclical Economic Forum the day before the *Barron's* article appeared that Saturday. He read of Gross's change of heart in *Barron's* just like other investors.

Gross said he had "no recollection" of what happened back then with McCulley, when he was asked about it in an e-mail interview. In an article in the *Orange County Register* in June 2002 Gross is said to have recoiled "at what he saw as a 'gutsy call.'" And while Gross did not scold McCulley for this forecast, the article said that Gross left McCulley "to stew in his own projection."[3]

It was clear to McCulley immediately that his forecast was no longer viable, even if he believed it. So his first step was to renounce it in the so-called Morning After summary of the Economic Forum, which he always writes. This was his first helping of crow—inside PIMCO.

In the summary, he said that the only issue with Federal Reserve policy was whether they would "take back" the four rate cuts made after 9/11 that reduced the target fed funds rate to 1.75 percent, from 3.5 percent.

McCulley, of course, was in the "no" camp, as he said in the Morning After memo, "on the notion that the Fed can't do a 'take back' without triggering the markets to romance a full-blown tightening process, which is fundamentally unjustified. Thus, I've argued that the FOMC would 'live with' the very low fed funds rate, because doing so would be the lesser of evils than trying to 'fix it.' "

But he said there now was no more need of any further discussion because "Bill Gross wisely ended any need for further debate on this matter, declaring in this morning's *Barron's* that a 3 percent fed funds rate by the end of 2002 is a 'reasonable' expectation." So, he concluded, "crow breakfast for me every day next week!"

McCulley's public recanting came in his "Fed Focus" column for April 2002, "Eating Crow With A Dr Pepper Chaser."

There are lots of fun things about being a talking head on TV, not the least of which is having people who ought to know better think that your IQ goes up when you go on the tube. It does not. The thing is sometimes called an Idiot Box for a reason. For example, on August 7, 2001, with the Fed targeting the Fed funds rate at 3.75 percent, I uttered the following line on CNBC: "Greenspan has tightened for the last time of his career."

The Fed funds rate is now 1.75 percent, and the Fed is openly threatening to "take back" the easing implemented after the September 11 Tragedy, when the Fed funds rate stood at 3.5 percent. Thus, I must eat those words spoken back on August 7, 2001: unless Chairman Greenspan retires soon, he is likely to tighten again in his career. And I must eat the words twice, because I foolishly reiterated them in the December 2001 "Fed Focus," written on November 28, 2001, when the Fed funds rate stood at 2 percent. Hubris is the handmaiden of human nature, and I'm as human as they come.

The story of McCulley's bold bet and what happened in the months following is more than a window on his relationship, at the time, with Gross and his other PIMCO colleagues. It also shows that what money managers think will happen does not always determine what they will do in the portfolios they manage. As we note in Chapter 8, there are two big steps to being a good investor or money manager: first, figuring out what you should do, and, second, acting on this knowledge. And this story shows that professionals, like Main Street investors, face difficulties in taking both of these steps.

Fuerbringer learned this lesson himself when he "worked" for a week as a currency trader at what was then Chase Manhattan Bank in August 1989. It was for a story, but Chase set up his trading so that it was as real as possible. By the end of the week, he had made a $167,686 profit, but his "boss" made clear he failed to make as much money as he should have because he did not push his good bets as hard as he should have.

Of course, the examples provided here are to make the case of how difficult it can be to take these two investing steps. Obviously, PIMCO's long-term success shows that more often than not its money managers are good at getting the right idea and putting it into practice.

PIMCO's marquee fund, the $99.8 billion Total Return Fund run by Gross, had outpaced the annual return of the other funds in its category by eight-tenths of a percentage point over the five years through 2006, according to Morningstar. McCulley's then $3.2 billion Short Term Fund has outdone the annual return of funds in his category by three-tenths of one percentage point in the same period. If that does not sound like a lot, remember that Gross's outperformance comes in a category that had an annual return of 4.4 percent, while McCulley's category had a return of 2.5 percent, according to Morningstar. So that is a 18.2 percent outperformance by Gross and 12 percent outperformance by McCulley.

And, of course, McCulley has been right about other things.

His Greenspan bet was based on his prediction that the then Fed chairman would be perfectly happy if the housing market bubbled up, and even over. And he was writing early on about the damage from the stock market bubble and the need for the Fed to slash interest rates aggressively to counter its damage. And while calling for big rate cuts, he predicted that the Fed would reduce its benchmark fed funds rate no lower than 0.75 percent. Fed policy makers stopped at 1 percent.

From an investor's point of view, this story shows that what a portfolio manager is saying publicly does not always make it to the bottom line. In other words, good bets do not always get made.

From a money manager's point of view, it is difficult to take these two investing steps because good ideas can get run over by the noise in the financial markets or by the competing views of their colleagues. In this case, the bond market was trading on the assumption that there were several rate increases by the Fed in the offing, and those believing otherwise were taking losses. That, at times, is the kind of pressure that changes even a correct forecast.

At mutual funds run like PIMCO, where there is an investment committee that sets pretty firm guidelines for all its portfolios, it may be even easier for a good idea to get overlooked.

PIMCO's investment committee, which is made up of seven permanent members—all partners—and one to three members who rotate on and off, lays out the essential bets, or risks, that it wants all of its portfolio managers to take, whether they are running mutual funds or accounts for private clients. Then each individual portfolio manager has a small bit of discretion around the target risk exposures established by the committee. As McCulley says, PIMCO "tries to deliver a homogeneous outlook as a firm. We do not have a star system; the system is the star."

So, knowing how a mutual fund company is run is important for investors when they choose where to put their money.

RUNNING ON CONSENSUS

We are going to tell you here how the bond bets are made at PIMCO. What they do in the bond world will sound complicated, because portfolio managers do not just go out and buy some bonds. But what they are doing is making the basic bond market bet: Will interest rates be going up or going down, and how fast is that likely to happen?

The investment committee's broad risk guidelines set the parameters for the bond bets that PIMCO's portfolio managers make in mutual funds and private accounts. Since performance at PIMCO is measured against fixed-income benchmarks, like the Lehman Brothers U.S. Aggregate Index, the risk guidelines either match those of the index benchmark or make a bigger bet than the index (that is, long the index) or make less of a bet than the index (that is, short the index).

The four broad risk guidelines are: duration, yield curve duration, spread duration, and volatility.

Duration. This is a measure of the time it takes for the owner of a bond to get back most of the money owed, including the principal and interest payments. Duration is always less than the maturity of a bond, except in the case of zero coupon bonds, where all payments are made at the time of maturity. A single bond has a duration and a whole portfolio of bonds has an overall duration, and this is the figure that is set by the PIMCO investment committee relative to the benchmark. Duration also is a measure of a bond's, or a portfolio's, sensitivity to a move in interest rates. The higher the duration, the bigger the move in the price of the bond when interest rates go up or down.

Yield Curve Duration. This is a measure of the sensitivity of a portfolio to changes in the shape of the yield curve. The yield curve is the range of maturities in the fixed-income market, from short, like the three-month Treasury bill, to long, like the 30-year Treasury bond. It usually slopes upward from short to long because investors want a higher yield to compensate them for the increased risk of lending for longer time periods. When the yield curve is steepening, the difference between the yield on the shortest-term security and the longest-term security is widening. When the yield curve is flattening, this difference is narrowing. When the yield curve is inverted, short-term rates are higher than longer-term rates. So, yield curve duration measures the value of the interaction of the moves of a series of interest rates.

A portfolio has positive yield curve duration when it is concentrated in securities with maturities in the 2-year to 10-year range, and it will do well if the yield curve steepens. This is because in a yield curve steepening, interest rates at the shorter end of the curve can fall, which pushes prices higher, improving performance. At the longer end of the curve, yields can rise, which pushes prices lower, reducing returns. A portfolio has a negative yield curve duration when its securities are concentrated in the 10-year to 30-year range, and it will do well if the yield curve flattens because the interest rate moves are the reverse of the yield curve steepening.

Spread Duration. This is a measure of the credit risk in the portfolio compared to the Treasury market, which is the safest part of the bond market. For example, as the spread—or difference—between yields on corporate bonds and yields on Treasury securities widens, the credit quality of corporate bonds is considered to be getting riskier, compared to Treasuries. If the investment committee thought this was an overreaction, it would adjust its spread duration to take advantage of an expected return of buyers to corporate bonds and the price increases that would follow.

Volatility. This is a measure of how much the price of a security might change over time. A security, or a portfolio, that is more volatile will move up or down in price more than a security, or portfolio, that is less volatile.

(Continued)

RUNNING ON CONSENSUS *(Continued)*

The volatility of a portfolio can be changed relative to its benchmark by buying or selling options on bonds. An option gives the buyer the right to purchase or sell an underlying security, like a bond, at a set price on a set date. But the buyer is not obligated to exercise the option. The seller of the option has the obligation to go through with the deal if the option is exercised. Because of this risk, the seller is paid for the option by the buyer.

Buying options reduces the volatility of the portfolio but also reduces its yield because of the cost of the options. Selling options increases the volatility of the portfolio but also increases its yield because of the premiums earned from selling the options. If you think volatility will be lower than is generally expected, you would sell options. If you think volatility will be higher than expected, you would buy options.

So, for example, an investment committee guideline for duration might say a half-year-long duration, plus or minus an eighth. That means the duration of the portfolio should be a half year longer than that of the benchmark. The extra half year of duration is a bet that interest rates will be falling, which means bond prices will be rising.

Portfolio managers have the discretion to either increase this half year to five-eighths of a year or reduce it to three-eighths of a year, depending on their own view of the market at the time.

On volatility, the investment committee might say sell enough volatility—options—to raise the stated yield of the portfolio half of a percentage point (50 basis points, in bond-land lingo) higher than the benchmark. The implied yield of the portfolio is increased by counting the premiums earned from selling the options. If volatility stays low, all the options sold expire without being exercised, and the portfolio gets to keep the profit from selling the options, which adds to its yield. If volatility picks up, however, some of the options will be exercised and the portfolio will have to deliver bonds to or buy bonds from the options buyer, which will reduce the yield of the portfolio.

The investment committee, which meets at least three times a week for over two hours, also sets a few other guidelines. One is for the extent of currency bets in portfolios investing in bonds abroad. Another is for so-called out-of-benchmark bets. For example, if there are no high-yield junk bonds in a benchmark for some portfolios, the investment committee can decide to add them to the portfolio anyway because it thinks that market is going to do very well.

At PIMCO a part of each portfolio manager's evaluation looks at the success the manager had with the small discretion they are allowed to diverge from the investment committee guidelines. The ratings for the portfolio managers are known as the Derby.

One conclusion that could be drawn from the investment committee approach at PIMCO is that Gross has been a money manager guided over the years more by consensus than by his own views, a fact that might surprise some other bond traders. McCulley agrees, but adds the caveat that "at the investment committee Gross can brute force something through if he chooses to. If Bill felt very strongly that a quarter-year-long was not enough for duration, he would simply look at us around the table and say, 'I take that on, but I am the chief investment officer and I am chairman of this committee and it is going to be a half-year-long duration.'" Gross is, McCulley said, a little like Greenspan in that he is an "autocratically congenial" leader of the investment committee at PIMCO.[4]

In the end, McCulley's forecast did not end up making any difference for PIMCO. He did not use the tiny discretion he had to change the tilt in his funds to benefit as much as possible from his view on the Fed and he did not influence the investment committee at PIMCO to alter the guidelines that it set for the mutual and private funds run by other money managers.

McCulley says this about that event: "I was long brains but short testicular fortitude."

If PIMCO had placed McCulley's Greenspan bet, holding durations long one year consistently, it would have increased the return on $1 billion by $2.1 million in the period from September 2001 to the end of March 2004, when the rate increases that began that June were fully incorporated into market expectations.

Gross himself has had his own difficulties in translating good ideas into investing strategies. In the fall of 1999 and again in early 2000, Gross had a chance to make a killing, but missed the opportunity.

This all took place during the now dreamlike time when federal budget deficits disappeared and were replaced by surpluses. With the surpluses, there was less need for the Treasury to issue new debt. In fact, the government was beginning to buy back older higher-interest-rate, longer-term bonds.

In early 2000, traders were pointing to Gross as the first big-time money manager to realize what the impact would be on the bond market of the Treasury's plan to buy back long-term government debt. It would send bond prices up, and quickly. His gobbling up of long-term Treasury securities for 21 days in late January and early February sent tremors through the bond market. But he and PIMCO had actually not done as well as they could have.

Gross began to buy his $8 billion of long-term Treasury bonds, bond futures, and zero coupon bonds on January 20, 2000. He should have started earlier, and he acknowledged this just a few weeks later in a story about him and these Treasury bets in *The New York Times*. The 20th of January was a full week after the Treasury announced that it was going to purchase—buy back—as much as $30 billion in long-term debt in the year 2000. In addition, the 20th of January was six months after it had become clear that government surpluses were going to force the government to start such buybacks in the future.

"I should have been shifting to that strategy long before January," Gross said at the time. He said that he had failed even to take his own advice, acknowledging that he had recommended buying Treasury securities in a newspaper article back in August 1999. "Why it took so long for me, or us, I have no idea," he said.[5]

McCULLEY'S BEST INVESTMENTS

There is no doubt that McCulley's best investment right now is his partnership in PIMCO, which has made him a wealthy man, with an annual income in the millions. But like most lucrative partnerships, there are golden handcuffs, which are designed to prevent partners from jumping from firm to firm. The handcuffs tie up part of a partner's wealth for a set number of years. And there is no relaxing for a partner, because PIMCO is very much a meritocracy, even at the partner level.

But it is only since he became a partner at PIMCO in January 2001 that his house has not been his biggest investment and asset.

He bought his first house, in Sherman Oaks, California, for $500,000 in 1988, when he was working at the Columbia Savings & Loan Association. The down payment for the purchase and the monthly mortgage nut stretched him and his then wife, Karen, so far that they did not have enough left for a washer, dryer, or refrigerator. So McCulley put them on his credit card.

To make matters worse, he had gotten a monthly adjustable-rate mortgage from Columbia as a way to decrease his initial mortgage payments. But the Fed began raising interest rates in the spring of 1988 and kept it up until late spring of 1989, raising its short-term benchmark rate as high as 9.75 percent, from 6.5 percent in February 1988. Adjustable-rate mortgages rose as high as 9.41 percent in April 1989, from 7.59 percent in February 1988, according to Freddie Mac. They slipped to 8.39 percent by the end of that year but rose again in the first half of 1990 before embarking on a downward path for two and three-quarter years.

He sold this house in 1993, after he had moved to New York to work as chief economist for UBS Securities. He had put another $100,000 into the California house, including improving the landscaping, pushing his basis up to $600,000. But the housing market was weak, because the economy was still sluggish in the aftermath of the 1990–1991 recession. He got only $415,000 and, with $390,000 left on the mortgage, he was worried he was going to have to write a check at the closing to pay off the last bit of mortgage. "It was my first serious investing experience and I lost a lot," he says.

He did not buy another house until 1996, in New Canaan, Connecticut. But that went well. And McCulley is no longer house poor or house rich, even though he paid $5 million for his house in Newport Coast, California, a home that is now valued at $7.5 million or more.

As of now he is looking to put more money into angel investing; a foundation named after the family's Netherlands Dwarf pet rabbit, Morgan le Fay; and a trust fund for his son, Jonnie. His first angel investment was in a private company of a friend, who still wants to keep McCulley's role under wraps. McCulley paid $250,000 to get 10 percent of this company and he is the only outside investor.

He is starting the Morgan le Fay Dreams Foundation with $1 million and plans to invest it conservatively, with the aim of replacing at least 5 percent each year, the minimum the foundation has to pay out in contributions to qualify for its special tax status. To compensate for inflation, this means the Dreams portfolio has to make 6.5 percent to 8 percent a year.

McCulley will have a core layer of Treasury Inflation Protected Securities, which are known as TIPS. These securities, like other Treasury securities, pay the investor a fixed rate of interest. But the rate is much lower than those of regular Treasuries of the same maturity. That is because the principals of TIPS increase along with the rise in the consumer price index, which is how the investor is compensated for a jump in the inflation rate. McCulley plans to have about 25 percent of his Dreams portfolio in TIPS because he wants an anchor of protection against nasty inflation, which he does not expect, but also knows cannot be ruled out. For him it is an example of being prepared for a low-probability occurrence that could have very big consequences.

McCulley will get some exposure to U.S. stocks through a value fund, like the one run by Bill Miller of Legg Mason Capital Management. Value funds focus on the search for overlooked and beaten-down stocks that the market has shunned but that should become darlings in the future. McCulley needs the stock exposure to get the growth in the Dreams portfolio necessary to preserve the principal, and it is in value funds that he thinks he can find his ten-baggers. About 25 percent of the portfolio will go here, with an emphasis on large-capitalization value stocks, not smaller ones.

The last big portion of the Dreams portfolio, about 30 percent, will go into an asset allocation fund, like that run by Robert Arnott of PIMCO. It is the first global asset allocation fund offered by PIMCO. It is a fund of funds that focuses on maintaining and growing real purchasing power through investments in other PIMCO funds, including those for real estate, commodities, emerging markets, high-yield junk bonds, and, of course, U.S. stocks and bonds. The point here is to improve returns by shifting among stocks, bonds, commodities, and real estate, and among sectors of those asset classes, when one looks better than another. This kind of tactical allocation is also a way to add more diversification to the Dreams portfolio.

Then there will be some bonds, but not too many, that McCulley will choose. They will most likely be in the high-yield junk bond sector, when it looks ripe for the picking.

The trust fund for McCulley's son is for the long haul. It does not have to produce any income for years and can suffer a lot of volatility. So it is a perfect place to add on risk, and McCulley intends to do that.

About 50 percent of this trust will be in emerging markets, our pick for the place to take on more risk. This is a bet on the long-term theme of globalization, a bet that emerging market countries become developed countries and, in the process, kick off a lot of profits for investors. This will happen as the risk of emerging markets is reevaluated, that is, reduced, which will raise the price-earnings ratios on stocks in those markets. On top of that, strong economic growth—stronger than that in developed countries—will add to the earnings and, therefore, the stock market gains. And, last, the currencies of emerging market countries will rise in value against the U.S. dollar, increasing the portfolio's gains when they are brought back home. But to get all of this, investors need to be there now, not later. Although the ride will be volatile, it will be profitable, just like the ride from high inflation to low inflation.

This transition to developed markets should also be good for bonds, so McCulley will put some of the emerging market portion of the trust into the fixed-income markets in these countries. And he will bet, until he is given a good reason to change his mind, on a further decline in the dollar. So he will not do any currency hedging.

Of the remaining 50 percent, about half would be in a Bill Miller–like value fund. The rest would be in health care—not hospitals, but something at the cutting edge of technology because that is another long-term play and a source of more tenbaggers. The health care portion would probably all be in the stock of U.S. companies.

McCulley's money, although his PIMCO partnership has vastly increased his net worth, is still pretty much in bonds, through his work, and real estate. He has never been a big stock man because until recently he says he did not have a net worth big enough to enable him to sleep well and not worry about providing for his family while the stock market was gyrating up and down.

Because he had been overweight real estate, he has been quite conservative in other places, with the exception of some 401(k) money in emerging markets.

"I've tended to be pretty well barbelled between real estate, which is the ultimate tangible asset, and being in the bond business," he said. "So my personal portfolio and my paycheck are theoretically inversely related, or hedged, you might say. If you get vibrant inflation, the value of my real estate is going to go up just fine. But bonds will be shunned and so the value of my PIMCO partnership will go down."

He believes that diversification matters not only in portfolios but also in a holistic way. So he has wanted to do something in his personal portfolio to hedge against his paycheck. "I am surprised how much company stock people buy because they are already long their company," he says.

"People say to me, 'Why not be in the bond market because you know so much about it?'" he added. "My answer is that I do not want—and cannot afford—to have too much of my net worth at risk if I happen to make a big mistake in the bond market. And, like it or not, mistakes do happen."

As for actual bonds, he has money in short-dated fixed-income securities, which he considers his liquidity, or cash. And when he becomes confident that interest rates have peaked globally, he will move some of that cash back into bonds—but only bonds outside of the United States, which give him a play on both the price increases when interest rates fall and on the currency gains.

As for real estate, he might buy some more, but not in California.

7

Speaking Of . . .

This is a collection of thoughts on how markets work and how thinking about those markets has changed. It is a primer that goes from the big thoughts of Adam Smith and John Maynard Keynes to lemons, of the automobile variety. It takes you from rough-and-tumble capitalism and free markets to political economics, and from the microeconomics of Smith to the macroeconomics of Keynes.

We show you that free markets need—and needed—government to work, so there is no economics, just political economics. We show how Keynes legitimatized the role of government in the economy by proving that investment boosts income. That led to government intervention with increased spending and tax cuts when private markets were weak and economic growth was slow or falling—and from there to big budget deficits.

We tell you about animal spirits and that investor behavior often is not planned at all, but just spontaneous, which is another reason why it is hard for Federal Reserve policy makers to know how their prescription for the economy will go down with the patient.

You will meet the man, Hyman Minsky, who figured out that stability is a fertile breeding ground for financial bubbles and see that in his analysis he called the good guys "hedge units." Managers of today's hedge funds have not been so lucky.

Since we are worried about the threat of deflation, we will look at how a deflationary episode would begin. Then will see what it took, belatedly, to bring it to an end in Japan and why the new chairman of the Federal Reserve, Ben S. Bernanke, does not think it will happen here.

We look at Pascal's Wager because it underlies advice from earlier in this book, that investors must worry about events that have a low probability but big negative consequences. We tell you that Joseph Schumpeter, a darling of Wall Street, has a secret. We question the predictive powers of the inverted yield curve. And we argue that the famous bond vigilantes were really not so powerful after all. They were empowered by Paul A. Volcker, who used them to his own end and pretty much fooled everybody into believing that budget deficits had more impact on interest rates than did monetary policy.

We also give you a sampling of Smith, Keynes, Minsky, and Bernanke in their own words. Their thoughts take a little effort to comprehend, but it is striking how clearly these economists make their points, despite using some jargon here and some jargon there. And, anyway, any investor who wants an edge should be familiar, a bit, with all of them.

All of this will help you understand better what is going on in financial markets in the big picture and the small picture.

SPEAKING OF THE INVISIBLE HAND . . .

Microeconomics starts with the presumption that Adam Smith's invisible hand of markets is not only always invisible, but also unfettered. His vision of free markets is founded on the proposition that buyers and sellers of goods and services are acting in their own best interest, willingly entering into exchange, without any coercion.

Here is how Smith put it in his *The Wealth of Nations*, published in 1776:

> *Every individual necessarily labours to render the annual revenue of the society as great as he can. He generally, indeed, neither intends to promote the public interest, nor knows how much he is promoting it. By preferring the support of domestic to that of foreign industry, he intends only his own security; and by directing that industry in such a manner as its produce may be of the greatest value, he intends only his own gain, and he is in this, as in many other cases, led by an invisible hand to promote an end which was no part of his intention. Nor is it always the worse for society that it was no part of his intention. By pursuing his own interest he frequently promotes that of the society more effectually than when he really intends to promote it. I have never known much good done by those who affected to trade for the public good.[1]*

So, microeconomics starts with the presumption that markets work best, for the individual and the society at large, when directed by the enlightened self-interest of market participants, without any interference from government.

It sounds good, but the world does not work this way, nor does microeconomics. That is because free-market microeconomics also starts with the presumption of the sanctity of private property rights. Without property rights, the invisible hand of markets would always be a hand in dispute, subject to arbitrary and capricious forearms.

Thus, even though the study of microeconomics is putatively either apolitical or nonpolitical, it has political roots: a government that defends private property through the rule of law and can take away property through the rule of law.

Economics is political because it is about the relationships between markets and peoples, within countries and between sovereign countries.

While most in business easily applaud Smith's invisible hand
of markets, it is much more difficult for many to applaud the visible fist of our collective will, as expressed by our government.
This should not be.

Democracy starts with the socialist notion of one person,
one vote. Accordingly, the democratic political process is inherently about equity: a struggle for justice in the distribution of
our collective economic pie, rather than the size of the pie itself. This exigency is in direct conflict with the cumulative voting system called capitalism, in which one dollar is accorded
one vote. The pursuit of profit, sometimes called greed, is the
energy directing Smith's invisible hand, with growth in our collective economic pie the time-proven result. The ethos of capitalism is, however, agnostic at best about whether the economic
pie is distributed justly and, more cynically, is antagonistic to
the idea. Democracy and capitalism are strange, and necessary,
fellow travelers: visible socialist ideals dueling with the invisible enigma of greed.

And this means that economics without politics is the analysis of a world that does not exist. Political economics is neither
an oxymoron nor a contradiction of terms, but a definition of
reality.

SPEAKING OF KEYNES . . .

When Keynes published *The General Theory* in 1936, he argued
that the conventional wisdom about the relationship of investment, savings, and interest rates was wrong. As he said at the
time, "The traditional analysis has been aware that saving de-
pends on incomes but it has overlooked the fact that income de-
pends on investment, in such fashion that, when investment
changes, income must necessarily change in just that degree

which is necessary to make the change in saving equal to the change in investment."[2]

This insight from Keynes, the first of three key ideas outlined here, was essentially the birth of macroeconomics, undermining the microeconomics-driven notion that savings drives investment. Quite to the contrary, Keynes argued: Investment drives income, and income drives savings. Thus, increased investment will beget increased income, which will, in the fullness of time, beget the necessary savings to pay for the increased investment.

Keynes' breaking of the analytical tyranny of the savings-equals-investment tautology was the basis for his advocacy of increased government investment, if private investment was insufficient to increase employment. And, in fact, that's what most of today's investment community knows about Keynes: that he was the man who legitimized illicit, intimate relations with budget deficits.

What Keynes actually did was legitimize clear thinking about macroeconomics, as distinct from microeconomics, demonstrating that what holds for the individual (Adam Smith's invisible hand) need not hold for an economic system. This principle is sometimes called the "fallacy of composition," and sometimes called the "paradox of aggregation." But we need not resort to fancy labels to define the common sense of macroeconomics. Anybody who's ever been a spectator at a crowded ball game has witnessed the difference between microeconomics and macroeconomics: from a micro perspective, it is rational for each individual to stand up to get a better view; but from a macro perspective, each individual acting rationally will produce the irrational outcome of everybody standing up, but nobody having a better view.

Put in a more direct economic way, while it can be rational for the individual to increase his or her propensity to save when facing hard times, the collective effect of all individuals trying to do so at the same time will be to ensure hard times.

Capitalism, as Keynes' contemporary Joseph Schumpeter intoned, is about entrepreneur-inspired investment. More specifically, capitalism flourishes where there is a will for investment—which brings us to Keynes' second seminal contribution to macroeconomic thought: Both the will and the wallet of capitalism are subject to the whims of the human spirit.

Of the will, Keynes wrote that "a large proportion of our positive activities depend on spontaneous optimism rather than on a mathematical expectation, whether moral or hedonistic or economic. Most, probably, of our decisions to do something positive, the full consequences of which will be drawn out over many days to come, can only be taken as a result of animal spirits—of a spontaneous urge to action rather than inaction, and not as the outcome of a weighted average of quantitative benefits multiplied by quantitative probabilities. Enterprise only pretends to itself to be mainly actuated by the statements in its own prospectus, however candid and sincere."

He then concluded that "if the animal spirits are dimmed and the spontaneous optimism falters, leaving us to depend on nothing but mathematical expectations, enterprise will fade and die; though fears of loss may have a basis no more reasonable than profits had before."[3]

Armed with the macroeconomic insight that the capitalist causal chain runs from investment to income to savings, not the other way around, Keynes enriched his analysis by observing that entrepreneurs are human beings, not a bunch of Adam Smithian invisible hands. Not exactly profound, you say, and you're right. But it is important to understand the straitjacket of the putative macroeconomics of the time, which was really nothing more than classical microeconomics in drag. After all, Secretary of the Treasury Andrew Mellon's advice in 1931 to President Herbert Hoover had been to "liquidate labor, liquidate stocks, liquidate the farmers, liquidate real estate. It will purge the rottenness out of the system. High costs of living and high living will come down. People will work harder, live a more moral life. Values will be adjusted, and enterprising people will pick up the wrecks from less competent people."[4]

Keynes was simply observing the consequences of Mellon's advice: Entrepreneurs who are being liquidated do not have the animal-spirited will to invest. In today's parlance, one might say that the Fed cannot push on a string; that is, its efforts to stimulate growth will not work if animal spirits are low.

Keynes also observed that they did not have the wallet to invest, which became the basis of Keynes' third seminal contribution to macroeconomics: that financial markets, notably the stock market, are both a boon and a bane to the capitalist process. Again, Keynes in his own words:

> *With the separation between ownership and management which prevails today and with the development of organized investment markets, a new factor of greater importance has entered in, which sometimes facilitates investment but sometimes adds greatly to the instability of the system. In the absence of security markets, there is no object in frequently attempting to revalue an investment to which we are committed. But the Stock Exchange revalues many investments every day and the revaluations give a frequent opportunity to the individual (though not to the community as a whole) to revise his commitments. It is as though a farmer, having tapped his barometer after breakfast, could decide to remove his capital from the farming business between 10 and 11 in the morning and reconsider whether he should return to it later in the week.*
>
> *But the daily revaluations of the Stock Exchange, though they are primarily made to facilitate transfers of old investments between one individual and another, inevitably exert a decisive influence on the rate of current investment. For there is no sense in building up a new enterprise at a cost greater than that at which a similar existing enterprise can be purchased; whilst there is an inducement to spend on a new project an extravagant sum, if it can be floated off on the Stock Exchange at an immediate profit.[5]*

So stock markets influence the investing and spending appetite—the animal spirits—of the people who are the engine of economic growth, the businesspeople who invest and the consumers who spend. Keynes was right long ago that stocks are a big factor among the variables that drive economic growth and would probably be one to want the Federal Reserve to worry more about stock bubbles when it is trying to moderate economic growth.

SPEAKING OF MINSKY . . .

Hyman Minsky is not a household name on Wall Street. But he should be, after the bubbles in stocks and housing. His huge contribution to macroeconomics was in his 1992 working paper, "The Financial Instability Hypothesis," which he said was an interpretation of Keynes' General Theory. Minsky's key addendum to Keynes' work was really quite simple: He provided a framework for distinguishing between stabilizing and destabilizing activity in financial markets. And, in the process, he made clear that long periods of stability can themselves lay the foundation for financial market bubbles and the period of instability that follows—in other words, what happened in the 1990s and what could happen again soon.

Here are excerpts from what Minsky wrote about his financial instability hypothesis in 1992 (note Minsky's good guys, the hedge units):

> *Three distinct income-debt relations for economic units, which are labeled as hedge, speculative, and Ponzi finance, can be identified.*
>
> *Hedge financing units are those which can fulfill all of their contractual payment obligations by their cash flows: the greater the weight of equity financing in the liability structure, the greater the likelihood that the unit is a hedge*

financing unit. Speculative finance units are units that can meet their payment commitments on "income account" on their liabilities, even as they cannot repay the principal out of income cash flows. Such units need to "roll over" their liabilities: (e.g., issue new debt to meet commitments on maturing debt). Governments with floating debts, corporations with floating issues of commercial paper, and banks are typically hedge units.

For Ponzi units, the cash flows from operations are not sufficient to fill either the repayment of principal or the interest due on outstanding debts by their cash flows from operations. Such units can sell assets or borrow. Borrowing to pay interest or selling assets to pay interest (and even dividends) on common stocks lowers the equity of a unit, even as it increases liabilities and the prior commitment of future incomes. A unit that Ponzi finances lowers the margin of safety that it offers the holders of its debts.

It can be shown that if hedge financing dominates, then the economy may well be an equilibrium-seeking and containing system. In contrast, the greater the weight of speculative and Ponzi finance, the greater the likelihood that the economy is a deviation-amplifying system. The first theorem of the financial instability hypothesis is that the economy has financing regimes under which it is stable, and financing regimes in which it is unstable. The second theorem of the financial instability hypothesis is that over periods of prolonged prosperity, the economy transits from financial relations that make for a stable system to financial relations that make for an unstable system.

In particular, over a protracted period of good times, capitalist economies tend to move from a financial structure dominated by hedge finance units to a structure in which there is large weight to units engaged in speculative and Ponzi finance. Furthermore, if an economy with a sizeable body of speculative financial units is in an inflationary state, and the authorities attempt to exorcise inflation by monetary constraint, then speculative units will become Ponzi units and the net worth of previously Ponzi units will quickly evaporate. Consequently, units with cash flow shortfalls will be forced to try to make positions by selling out positions. This is likely to lead to a collapse of asset values.[6]

Minsky passed away in 1996, just as the financing patterns of the new economy were following precisely his script, moving progressively toward Ponzi units. Then the Federal Reserve declared that inflation was a threat and moved to contain prices by raising interest rates. And, lo and behold, the Ponzi finance units evaporated and speculative finance units morphed into Ponzi units. Risk asset prices collapsed and the bubble burst.

SPEAKING OF SCHUMPETER . . .

Joseph Schumpeter, the author of *Capitalism, Socialism and Democracy* (Harper & Brothers, 1942), coined the phrase "creative destruction" to describe the nature of entrepreneur-driven capitalism. It means that the price of technological innovation, which drives long-term economic growth, is that established technologies and their companies are driven out of business. The rediscovery of this clever phrase lifted Schumpeter to the lofty status of Wall Street's favorite dead economist in the 1990s. Wall Street needed an economic theory to justify paying unsustainable prices for NASDAQ stocks, and found one: Keynes is dead, long live Schumpeter.

What few on Wall Street seem to know is that Schumpeter also believed that capitalism would ultimately morph into socialism, as the prosperity wrought by creative destruction would breed a class of idle intellectuals (yes, Schumpeter's words) who would stop it. So, we have the odd happenstance of Wall Street celebrating the work of a scholar forecasting the demise of Wall Street, which just adds credence to a long-held belief that many on Wall Street—and elsewhere—quote dead scholars they have never actually read.

SPEAKING OF DEFLATION . . .

Deflation occurs when prices of goods and services actually fall, as opposed to disinflation, which happens when the pace of price increases slows down.

But a bout of deflation, which would be highlighted by declines in the closely watched consumer price index (CPI) and the producer price index (PPI) for finished goods, is not likely to start that way. Instead, price deflation is likely to be preceded by another kind of deflation: debt deflation. And that is when the Federal Reserve has to act to prevent the debt deflation meltdown from turning into a period of price deflation.

A debt deflation meltdown is a self-feeding fall in the market value of assets, like stocks and bonds, relative to the cost of the debt, or borrowing, assumed to acquire them. It can be triggered by a shock, by a regulatory regime shift, or simply by the exhaustion of a bubble, when greed gives way to fear.

This decline in asset value makes lenders fear they will not be paid back. So they demand that any maturing debt be paid off, rather than rolled over into new debt. But this demand for immediate repayment would, in effect, force the borrowers to liquidate themselves, as they rush to sell off their assets in a falling market.

In a falling market, however, that's damned difficult for individual borrowers, and impossible for the community of borrowers, with everybody rushing for the door at the same time.

But the very fact that it is impossible for the community to liquidate all its debts by selling all its assets (you have to have somebody to sell to) reinforces the incentive for individual lenders to demand that individual borrowers liquidate themselves as quickly as possible, so they can get paid something before prices fall even more.

This individually rational (microeconomic) but collectively irrational (macroeconomic) behavior is, of course, the stuff of bank runs—nasty self-feeding things, as George Bailey found out in *It's a Wonderful Life.*

In the language of finance, the run dynamic is called systemic risk, and, fortunately, we have designed mechanisms to help defuse such runs: deposit insurance for bank deposits, and the Federal Reserve, with its role as the lender of last resort through its discount window, at which banks can get hard, cold cash for their loan and security portfolios.

Indeed, the banking system itself is an additional prophylactic against debt deflation in the capital markets because it is the place solid companies turn to for loans when they are unable to roll over their maturing debt. In fact, contingent commitments by the banking system to lend to companies are an integral part of most companies' ability to actually sell bonds in the capital markets. Buyers of company debt demand that issuers have a bank backup line of credit for rolling over maturing debt, as an insurance policy against forced liquidation in the event that the bond market is caught in a bout of infectious risk aversion.

Most elementally, the capital markets and the bank lending market are complements, not substitutes. They need each other. Banks need the bond market to determine, in real time, the appetite for risk, and at what price. The bond market needs banks to act as a conduit for the Fed's lender-of-last-resort function—the circuit breaker—in case the capital markets are caught in a paroxysm of remorse after an inflationary bubble in asset prices.

And if the banking system cannot, or will not, play that role, as was the case in the Depression, then a debt deflation meltdown will beget a more generalized deflation in goods and services prices—with the CPI and the PPI actually declining—as economic activity grinds to a halt.

Thus, when thinking about deflationary risk, as all right-thinking risk takers should be doing at a time when inflation is in check and the next deflationary threat is just a recession away, it is very important to think first in terms of deflation in asset prices—of debt deflation. That is because such debt deflation is the proximate cause of the rising risk of actual deflation in the prices of goods and services.

Accordingly, policy authorities cannot wait for deflation in goods and services prices before beginning their fight against deflation. The time to act is when debt deflation threatens the private sector arrangements of lenders and borrowers.

SPEAKING OF DEFLATION AND JAPAN . . .

Debt deflation in Japan should never have happened. And it would never have if Japanese policy makers had pursued and sustained proper Keynesian reflationary policies following the collapse of the equity and property bubbles in the early 1990s. But they did not choose to do this, partly because of stubbornness, partly because of a lack of policy coordination, and partly because of the inability to reach a consensus on what was the right policy to pursue to deal with deflation and Japan's other economic problems, including its troubled banking system.

The Japanese did not begin to act in a concerted way to bring an end to their deflation until March of 2001, with a policy that was called quantitative easing (QE).

You need not be an economist to grasp the essence of the approach. Quantitative easing was simply a fancy way for the Bank of Japan to commit resolutely to subordinate Japan's monetary policy to her fiscal policy, despite the Bank of Japan's legal independence from Japan's elected government.

Effectively, the Bank of Japan promised to fund, at a zero interest rate, any and all of the government debt issued to cover the budget deficits that were being used to stimulate economic growth. That growth, in turn, would eventually provide the rising price pressures that would bring an end to deflation. (This is very similar to what the Fed promised to do to help the U.S. government pay for the cost of World War II, as we noted in Chapter 4. But there was no deflation threat at the time. It was the opposite. The government had to put price controls into place in the United States to help contain inflation.)

There were two important components of Japan's antideflation policy: One is that the Bank of Japan adjusted its policy to the needs of the government. The second is that the Bank of Japan, by keeping interest rates at zero by purchasing much of the debt issued by the government, prevented the rise in interest rates that would normally be associated with the growth the government was stimulating with its deficits. The Bank of Japan's purchases of longer-term Japanese government bonds averaged $28 billion per quarter, in dollar terms, from April 2001 through March 2006.

Such a rise in interest rates, if allowed, would have just offset the stimulus impact of the deficits, undermining the antideflation program.

Bank of Japan bond buying also included the debt the government issued to raise the billions of yen it needed to intervene in the currency market to buy dollars to prevent the yen from rising in value against the dollar. These dollar-buying sprees crested at $138 billion in the first quarter of 2004.

A rise in the value of the yen had to be prevented. If it was not, Japanese exports, which were the engine needed to get the Japanese economy going again, would have become more expensive and less competitive abroad, reducing the stimulus they could bring to economic growth.

The Bank of Japan promised to persevere in this policy until the consumer price index was rising, year on year, at a sustainable pace. It took time and some other necessary fixes, including recapitalizing the deflation-ravaged banking system. The Bank of Japan bought up to $8 billion, in dollar terms, of asset-backed securities as a way to substitute for the nonfunctioning banking system and supplement the undeveloped capital market. But the reflationary policy worked and the Japanese were able to announce the end of quantitative easing in March 2006.

SPEAKING OF DEFLATION AND BERNANKE . . .

Bernanke has said that the cooperation between a country's central bank and its government is a key component of any plan to fight deflation. It is important, Bernanke said in a speech in Japan in 2003, to recognize that an independent central bank has a different role in a deflationary environment than it has in an inflationary environment. When facing the threat of inflation—and the threat that excessive money creation would increase inflationary pressures—Bernanke said that "the virtue of an independent central bank is its ability to say 'no' to the government. With protracted deflation, however, excessive money creation is unlikely to be the problem, and a more cooperative stance on the part of the central bank may be called for. Under the current circumstances, greater cooperation for a time between the Bank of Japan and the fiscal authorities is in no way inconsistent with the independence of the central bank, any more than cooperation between two independent nations in pursuit of a common objective is inconsistent with the principle of national sovereignty."[7]

Bernanke went on to say that such cooperation, despite the temporary subordination of the independence of the Bank of Japan, "could help solve the problems that each policy maker faces on its own. Consider for example a tax cut for households and businesses that is explicitly coupled with incremental BOJ [Bank of Japan] purchases of government debt—so that the tax cut is in effect financed by money creation."

You can get a feel for what Bernanke might do in the United States from the advice that he gave to the Japanese in May 2003. It is, in effect, what Milton Friedman, the famous monetarist who died in 2006, dubbed a helicopter drop of money. And it does give you confidence that Bernanke is prepared.

In Japan, Bernanke said that he would want a very robust reflation target—one that would pretty much guarantee that deflation would not recur. The inflation increases sought during the reflation period would be higher than a normal inflation target. He would also seek to make up the price gains lost during the period of deflation by assuming a 1 percent inflation rate in each year there were actual price decreases. "One might argue that the legal objective of price stability should require not only a commitment to stabilize prices in the future but also a policy of actively reflating the economy, in order to restore the price level that prevailed prior to the prolonged period of deflation," Bernanke said in his speech.

He went on to say:

> *What I have in mind is that the Bank of Japan would announce its intention to restore the price level (as measured by some standard index of prices, such as the consumer price index excluding fresh food) to the value it would have reached if, instead of the deflation of the past five years, a moderate inflation of, say, 1 percent per year had occurred. (I choose 1 percent . . . because a slightly positive average rate of inflation reduces the risk of future episodes of sustained deflation.) Note that the proposed price-level target is a moving target, equal in the year 2003 to a value approximately 5 percent above the actual price level in 1998 and rising 1 percent per year thereafter. Because deflation implies falling prices while the target price level rises, the failure to end deflation in a given year has the effect of increasing what I have called the price-level gap. The price-level gap is the difference between the actual price level and the price level that would have obtained if deflation had been avoided and the price stability objective achieved in the first place.*
>
> *A successful effort to eliminate the price-level gap would proceed, roughly, in two stages. During the first stage, the inflation rate would exceed the long-term desired inflation rate, as the price-level gap was eliminated and the effects of previous deflation undone. Call this the reflationary phase of policy. Second, once the price-level target was reached, or nearly so, the objective for policy would become a conventional inflation target or a price-level target that increases over time at the average desired rate of inflation.*[8]

Most important, Bernanke is not worried about the problems Japan had in fighting deflation or the time it took. It is his belief that deflation will not happen here, and if it does, the Fed can deal with it.

"I do not view the Japanese experience as evidence against the general conclusion that U.S. policy makers have the tools they need to prevent, and, if necessary, to cure a deflationary recession in the United States," he said in his famous printing press speech in November 2002.

If deflation occurred, he said, a "broad-based tax cut, for example, accommodated by a program of open-market purchases to alleviate any tendency for interest rates to increase, would almost certainly be an effective stimulant to consumption and hence to prices."[9] In other words, the Fed would keep interest rates from rising as the tax cut stimulated spending, growth, and, eventually, price increases.

SPEAKING OF LEMONS . . .

The market for lemons helps explain why your car loses 20 percent to 30 percent when you drive it out of the dealer's lot and it becomes a used car. This theory, which won Professor George Akerlof of the University of California at Berkeley the Nobel Memorial Prize in Economic Science in 2001, also tells you why a lot of emerging market stocks and bonds might be underpriced and therefore a good bargain if you or a good money manager can do enough homework.

In the used car market, potential buyers of your car presume that you know more about the car than they do, including whether or not it is a lemon. This informational asymmetry about the quality of the car leads buyers to reduce the price they are willing to pay for used cars to compensate for their lack of knowledge and the chance that they may get a lemon.

A lot of money managers who invest in emerging markets outperform the overall market, as measured by an index, by exploiting the market for lemons thesis: know your cars—or emerging market stocks and bonds—on a micro basis, thereby affording yourself the opportunity to exploit the market's macro presumption of informational asymmetries. In other words, there should be a lot of value there for the finding.

This picking among the potential lemons, however, may be getting less profitable as emerging markets become more and more easy to invest in. The easier they are to invest in, the more money they will attract from index and other funds that just want to be there. And that indiscriminate buying could make some of the good values too expensive.

SPEAKING OF AN INVERTED YIELD CURVE . . .

One of the signals that a recession is in the offing has been the inversion of the yield curve. The yield curve is the range of interest rates on Treasury securities, from short-term to long-term. It usually slopes upward, with longer-term interest rates higher than shorter-term interest rates. That is natural because investors want to be paid a higher interest rate for longer-term securities to compensate them for the added risk of lending their money over longer periods.

When shorter-term interest rates are higher than longer-term interest rates, the yield curve is inverted. One of the reasons that an inverted yield curve can signal that a recession is ahead is that short-term interest rates have been pushed higher than longer-term rates by the Fed, as it raised its short-term interest rate benchmark to slow economic growth and to contain inflation. In the past, as periods of Fed tightening to curb inflation had inverted the yield curve they had often also led to recessions.

Traditionally, the yield curve was inverted when the yield on the three-month Treasury bill was higher than the yield on the 30-year bond. When the 30-year bond was discontinued in 2001, the focus moved to the three-month bill and the 10-year note. But many on Wall Street just watch the yield on the 2-year note and the 10-year note.

One reason the yield curve is not an effective forecasting tool anymore is because inflation is stable and interest rates are historically low. In this environment, investors will take more risk. So when Fed policy makers are raising rates to slow economic growth, investors still are buying longer-term Treasury securities to get the higher return because they are not worried about inflation. But this buying keeps longer-term interest rates from rising, and that does two things. It means the Fed rate increases are less of a drag on growth—making a recession less likely—and they allow the yield curve to be inverted more easily.

Alan Greenspan also thinks that the inverted yield curve is no longer a good predictor of recessions. Here is what he said in an exchange with Senator Richard Shelby, Republican of Alabama, on July 21, 2005, according to the transcript from Bloomberg of the hearing before the Committee on Banking, Housing, and Urban Affairs:

> *It is certainly the case that, if you go back historically, that an inverted yield curve has actually been a reasonably good measure of potential recession in front of us. The quality of that signal has been declining in the last decade, in fact, quite measurably.*
>
> *And the reason, basically, is that it was a good measure in the early period when banks, commercial banks, were the major financial intermediaries. And when you had long-term interest rates rise—I should say, short-term interest rates rise relative to long-term interest rates—it usually implied a squeeze on the profitability of commercial banks because they tend to hold somewhat longer maturities on the asset side of the balance sheet than on the liability side.*
>
> *And as a consequence of that, that squeeze was usually associated with an economy running into some trouble.*
>
> *But we have had extraordinary new avenues of financial intermediation developed over the last decade and a half. And therefore, there are innumerable other ways in which savings can move into investment without going through the commercial banks.*

*And as a result, a straightforward statistical analysis of
the efficacy of the issue of yield inversion as a forward tool—
I should say that the evidence very clearly indicates that its
efficacy as a forecasting tool has diminished very dramatically because of economic events.*

But whereas Greenspan said that the yield curve's forecasting
prowess had diminished very dramatically, he did not say that it
had fallen to zero. And that is why recession concerns surfaced
when the yield curve inverted in 2006, for the first time since
2000.

SPEAKING OF DEFICITS AND VIGILANTES . . .

So where have all the bond vigilantes gone? In the 1980s, when
federal budget deficits rose to record levels during the Reagan administration and the fight against inflation was just picking up
steam, the bond vigilantes would swoop in and push interest rates
higher anytime there was a threat of deficits getting bigger.

In the beginning of the 1990s, the bond vigilantes—a moniker
invented by economist Edward Yardeni—had enough clout to
convince the newly elected President Clinton that cutting the federal budget deficit was more important than an economic stimulus program, which would have swelled the deficit.

James Carville, the swaggering aide to the candidate and President Clinton, often joked on the lecture circuit that he had
dropped his wish to be reincarnated as a baseball player with a
.400 batting average. Now he wanted to come back as the bond
market, which would allow him to intimidate everyone.

Well, these bond vigilantes have not been around since the
surpluses generated in the Clinton administration became deficits
again after President George W. Bush's tax cuts, a recession, and
the wars in Afghanistan, Iraq, and the fight against terrorism. In
fact, as the deficit rose, longer-term interest rates pretty well held
their ground.

The retreat of the bond vigilantes is a signal that they were not as important as we—Fed watchers, financial analysts, money managers, and journalists—had believed. Monetary policy is more important than fiscal policy (read deficits) in determining the path of interest rates. So the bond market vigilantes do not rule the world. In fact, they reign only when the Fed chooses to let them reign. And that's what the Fed did under Volcker. In academic terms, this "bond vigilante" paradigm is all about monetary policy dominating fiscal policy. With Volcker, it was about diverting attention from what the Fed was doing.

Volcker wanted to tame inflation. To do that he had to use the brute force of interest rates to slow economic growth. But rising deficits were stimulating growth, making his efforts more difficult. Volcker could have explained this. But as a matter of political marketing, it was much easier for the Fed to hide under the cover of the bond vigilantes, saying that their fear of deficits was the reason for the higher longer-term interest rates.

In the 1980s, Fed watchers and reporters would all sit right behind Volcker in the hearing room, watching and smelling him smoke cigar after cigar, while listening to him repeatedly tell members of Congress that there were only two questions that mattered, and the answer to both was the same. The questions were why are interest rates still high when inflation is falling, and why can not or will not the Fed bring down all interest rates by cutting short-term interest rates?

Volcker's answer always was: because the budget deficit is too big. Inflation might be falling, he would allow, but inflationary expectations were being held up, he'd argue, because of budget deficits, and the associated concern that Uncle Sam would, ultimately, print money to pay for them. In turn, such elevated inflationary expectations were, he'd preach, holding up long-term interest rates.

Therefore, he'd opine, the Fed couldn't bring down long-term rates simply by cutting short-term interest rates. Indeed, lower short-term rates could, in the context of excessive budget deficits, actually generate higher, not lower, long-term rates, he'd thunder, as Fed accommodation of excessive budget deficits would simply reinforce the inflationary expectations begotten by such excessive budget deficits.

After hearing Volcker, all the Wall Streeters would rush out to the pay phones in the hall and call their offices or trading floors, relaying that Volcker was very hawkish and, therefore, traders and investors should sell bonds. Budget deficits were bad, very bad, Volcker had said, and if he said it, Wall Street was not going to argue with him.

After all, it was the duty of the bond market to impose discipline on those nasty deficit spenders. And all these Wall Streeters following Volcker were part of the band of bond vigilantes that Volcker had let believe that they were even more powerful than he and the Fed, as long as budget deficits were not under control.

It really was a simple syllogism: Fiscal deficits determine long-term inflation expectations, which are a more powerful force than short-term interest rates in the determination of long-term interest rates. In real time, it didn't matter whether it was true. If enough people believed it was true, and Volcker acted as if it were true— refusing to cut short-term interests unless and until Congress cut those damnable deficits—then it was true for trading purposes.

Trading is not about truth, but about staying ahead of the consensus perception of truth. But perception is reality only until reality bites perception in the backside, as it repeatedly does when it comes to the thesis that fiscal policy dominates monetary policy in the determination of long-term interest rates. It simply isn't true.

Long rates have moved in the same direction as short rates a majority of the time over the past 25 years. Long rates have moved less than short rates, to be sure, with the yield curve flattening when the Fed is tightening, and steepening when the Fed is easing. But the direction of long-term rates has been dominated by the direction of short-term rates, under the monopoly control of the Fed, despite their partial revolt in the tightening cycle of 2004 to 2006. And the dominant determinant of short-term rates has been the pace of economic growth.

Yes, it is probably true that budget deficits make long-term interest rates structurally higher than otherwise would be the case—absolutely and relative to short-term interest rates.

But fiscal policy as an active tool of countercyclical business cycle management is inherently impotent if monetary policy authorities are unwilling to accommodate such use of fiscal policy. So, the bond vigilantes will not be onstage again until the Fed wants them.

SPEAKING OF PASCAL'S WAGER . . .

This is all about the relationship of risk to the consequences of taking that risk. The idea is a very important concept in managing an economy and in investing. In his *Pensees*, written in the seventeenth century, Blaise Pascal argued that it was wiser to believe in God than not to. "Let us weigh the gain and the loss in wagering that God is," Pascal wrote. "Let us estimate these two chances. If you gain, you gain all; if you lose, you lose nothing. Wager, then, without hesitation that He is."

In this case, you have little to lose if you believe in God and God does not exist, but you have a great deal to lose if you do not believe in God but God does exist. In economics and investing, Pascal's Wager has come to mean that it is not a good idea to ignore a very small risk that could have very great consequences. When you check with your boss about a decision you have made, even if you are pretty sure the boss will say yes, you are heeding Pascal's advice.

The same was true for Fed policy makers when they went into action immediately when there was just a whiff of a threat of deflation. Ignoring that small threat, even though the likelihood of actual deflation was small, could have had enormously negative consequences for the economy. Pascal's Wager is also good advice for investors, because it tells them that some hedges in their portfolio are not a bad idea, especially when everything in financial markets appears to be going in the right direction.

SPEAKING OF THE LONG TERM . . .

There is your long term, which means sticking with it. The basic idea is that over the long term, 10 or 20 years, the ups and downs in a market even out and since most of us are not good market timers, it pays to stay put. But professional money managers, and the financial markets in general, have a different notion of long-term investing.

Returns are the reward for taking real risk, notably the risk that you lose hard cold dollars relative to parking your wealth in a money-market account.

The sources of risk on investments are many and varied: duration risk, equity risk, credit risk, volatility risk, yield curve risk, liquidity risk, and, yes, even fraud risk.

The longer the period for which you underwrite these risks, the greater is the uncertainty associated with underwriting them. Accordingly, basic logic says that the longer the time horizon for underwriting investment risk, the greater should be the expected real return.

Conceptually, there should not be any controversy about that. It's just common sense, similar to a car manufacturer demanding that you pay up at an increasing rate for extra years or miles on the warranty—the longer the horizon, the greater is the uncertainty associated with bad stuff happening. In the financial markets, such extra return for taking risks is frequently called excess return.

But this is not the way most money managers work. They are more interested in a shorter time period and are not that concerned with the real underlying value of an investment in a stock or bond. Why? Because they are focused on what the market as a whole thinks of the value of an investment, not what the actual worth of the investment is over the long term.

This is not a new game. Indeed, none other than Keynes described it beautifully in Chapter 12 of *The General Theory*.

The professional investor and speculator, he wrote, are not in-

terested in calculating correctly the potential yield of an investment over its lifetime. All they want to know is "what the market
will value it at, under the influence of mass psychology, three
months or a year hence." He called this "the conventional basis
of valuation," and said the professional and the speculator are
only interested in how this valuation will change "a short time
ahead of the general public."

Keynes did not dismiss this approach. Rather, he said that
"it is not sensible to pay 25 for an investment of which you believe the prospective yield to justify a value of 30, if you also
believe that the market will value it at 20 three months
hence."[10]

So foreseeing change in "the conventional basis of valuation" is the cat's meow of professional investment management.
The horizon that is relevant to the modern-day investment
manager varies, depending on many factors, including the
type of investment vehicle and the track record. For an established investment manager like PIMCO, let's say three to five
years.

SPEAKING OF BEER AND OIL . . .

As a philosophical matter, economists hate cartels (except for the
ones that demand a PhD to be considered for certain jobs and
the tenure system). Cartels are bad, you are taught, because they
lead to lower output and higher prices than otherwise would be
the case.

For example, the cartel that runs the beer and hot dog business at a major league sports event clearly sells fewer brews and
fewer dogs, and at much higher prices, than would be the case in
a world of competition. Why, then, do cartels exist? Why can't
government outlaw them?

In the matter of suds and wieners, the answer is easy: The
government, otherwise known as the owner of the stadium, runs

the cartel. And the government, because in most cases it owns the stadium, is financing it at municipal bond rates and is leasing it to the private sector. Thus, the government has the right—the property right—to decide who can and can't provide refreshments for America's pastime.

Theoretically, we the people could object to this cartel, demanding that local governments bring competition to the provision of a warm beer and a cold hot dog. But we don't, for reasons that are not clear. We just don't. It could be that we the people intuitively understand that it is better that beer be expensive at the ball park, as a prophylactic against the externality of drunk driving on the way home from the game. But that's just a hunch; and, in any event, this is hardly a matter of great national or international economic importance.

Not so, of course, in the matter of oil, which is similarly controlled by a cartel called the Organization of Petroleum Exporting Countries (OPEC). The low-cost producer, Saudi Arabia, is the marginal producer, also sometimes known as the swing producer.

This is not the way it is supposed to be, at least according to textbook microeconomics, which teaches that the supply curve for a commodity is upward sloping, with the highest-cost producer serving as the marginal producer. Why doesn't this hold in the matter of oil?

It's very simple: Saudi Arabia is a sovereign country, blessed by the divinity with huge pools of oil, easier to get out of the ground than water. And Saudi Arabia exercises its sovereignty by limiting production, even though it could handily underprice other producers of oil that have higher production costs. Thus, the economics of oil is inherently political economics: It is impossible, literally impossible, to forecast oil prices without making an assumption about how Saudi Arabia will exercise its sovereign property right in the oil below its surface and how other sovereign nations will or won't respect Saudi Arabia's sovereignty.

SPEAKING OF OTHERWISE . . .

When something changes in financial markets, analysts, investors, and journalists always want to know what the change
means. Will stocks go up? Will stocks go down? Will interest
rates go up or down? But quite often, the best forecast is not up
or down. It is that stocks, or interest rates, will not go up—or
down—as much as they would have otherwise.

8

Driving Your Portfolio

"**D**riving Your Portfolio" is about making investment adjustments as you negotiate the difficult curves in the changing financial environment ahead.

The first step is coming up with ideas. This book has aimed to help with that, pointing out the need to take on more risk, delving into diversification, assessing what could go wrong in markets in the future, spelling out how to watch the Fed, and exploring tidbits of economic and financial market lore. The second step, putting ideas into practice, is much harder. As we showed in Chapter 6, having good ideas and acting on them is not easy, even for the professionals.

It would be nice to have one solution for all investors, but the differences in investor behavior make that impossible. Investing for the long term is a good idea, especially in stocks. But diversifying into bonds and commodities is smart for many investors, even though the authors have an obvious bias for bonds. So is adjusting your portfolio to play a trend, like a nice run in stocks or a rebound in the junk bond market. So we suggest all these adjustments—and more—in the hope that they will lead more investors to actually act, so they will get better returns in the future.

The biggest adjustment investors have to make in the years ahead is to add risk to their portfolios, and the first part of this chapter is about the markets where that extra risk can be picked up. While we have a favorite market to turn to, we are not advocating a single-bullet solution. Risk can be added to portfolios in many ways and in many degrees. The important thing is to add risk to your portfolio, even if you do not go whole hog.

In line with watching the Federal Reserve, there are adjustments that can be made in your portfolio when the Fed is tightening and easing. The monthly manufacturing index reported by the Institute for Supply Management, which we introduced you to in Chapter 4, will help in the timing of these tune-ups.

We also think that Treasury Inflation Protected Securities, or TIPS, have a role in portfolios as a hedge against an inflation mistake and as part of a diversification strategy.

We will take a look at what one could do as interest rates move as China unravels the peg of its currency to the dollar.

Until the current account deficit is brought under control, the dollar should be in a downward tilt. So there is a reason to adjust your portfolio to take advantage of that opportunity.

We also tackle what investors should do if there is a bout of deflation. We do not expect it, but it seems fair to discuss it briefly, if we are also going to contemplate, in the TIPS section, the possibility of a jump in inflation.

MARKETS FOR RISK

Emerging markets are at the top of our list of the markets where there is more risk for the taking. They are at the far end of the risk spectrum. They are in transition from mass-producer to consumer-driven markets, a change that will make their economies vibrant, adding to the returns of their stock markets. And, as we noted in Chapter 1, they can offer a better return, based on historical data, with only a slightly higher risk level than other alternatives. It is a long-term bet—a decade, maybe more—but it is the way to go.

These markets got their name in 1981 when Antoine Van Agtmael of the International Finance Corporation (IFC) was promoting the idea of investing in markets that were located in what were then called third world countries. In coming up with a snappy name for one of these new funds, he hit on Emerging Markets Growth Fund. It caught on.[1]

There is no simple definition of these countries, which can be seen in Figure 8.1. But many countries have been emerging markets, even if they were not called that, at one time or another. In the 1800s, the United States was an emerging market that attracted European investors to buy stocks and bonds in the railroads. Russia was an emerging market at the beginning of the nineteenth century and is one again today.

Under a broad definition used by the index and credit-rating company Standard & Poor's, a market is considered emerging if

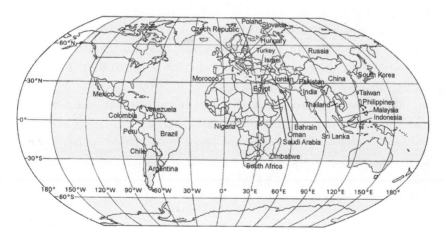

FIGURE 8.1 Emerging Markets Worldwide

There are 33 emerging markets where investors can increase their risk and return.

Source: Data from MSCI and Standard & Poor's.

it is located in a low- or middle-income economy, does not require enough financial disclosure, has laws that discriminate against foreign investors, or does not have a strong regulator to watch over financial markets.[2]

One or all of these reasons qualify a market as emerging and help explain why they are more risky and have traditionally been markets hard for individual investors to get into on their own.

The emerging markets index compiled by MSCI has 27 countries: Argentina, Brazil, Chile, China, Colombia, Czech Republic, Egypt, Hungary, India, Indonesia, Israel, Jordan, Malaysia, Mexico, Morocco, Pakistan, Peru, Philippines, Poland, Russia, South Africa, South Korea, Sri Lanka, Taiwan, Thailand, Turkey, and Venezuela. Standard & Poor's adds Bahrain, Nigeria, Oman, Saudi Arabia, Slovakia, and Zimbabwe to the list, for a total of 33.

It is quite a varied list. Zimbabwe has an economy less than a third of the size of Montana's. China is the world's fourth largest economy, has a space program, will host the Olympics in 2008, is a permanent member of the United Nations Security Council, and is a major trading partner with the United States.

Yet China fits the emerging market definition because it still has restrictions on capital flows into and out of the country and on the buying of stocks. Its currency, the yuan, is not freely traded. Its banking system is just developing, and there is not enough disclosure of financial data.

These factors have made it difficult to pick and choose what to buy in China and may have played into its poor performance, despite strong economic growth, relative to other emerging market countries over the past decade. In the 10 years through December of 2006, the compound annual rate of return for the MSCI China index was a loss of 3.4 percent, the fifth worst performance among the 27 emerging market countries in the MSCI index. The compound annual return over the same 10 years for all these emerging markets was a gain of 6.7 percent, while the compound annual return for Far Eastern emerging markets was a decline of 1 percent.

Ten or 15 years ago, we would have mentioned emerging markets only as an exotic place for retail or individual investors to put some—very little—of their money, and only if they had a high risk tolerance. We would also have reminded investors of one of the rules of thumb back then: If a particular emerging stock market had a good year, which was just the thing that would attract new investors, it was likely that the next year would be a bad one. That was how volatile these markets were.

But emerging markets can be approached with a different attitude now. While there are still reasons to be wary—such as the sudden and swift 24.5 percent sell-off in 2006 from May 8 to June 13—emerging markets are less emerging these days than they used to be. In fact, they rebounded quickly from the 2006 sell-off. And investors need to get some of the risk and return these markets offer.

The last major crisis in emerging markets—a roller-coaster ride to remember—began when Thailand devalued its currency in 1997, starting a selling stampede. Russia then defaulted on its debt in 1998, Turkey devalued its currency, and Argentina defaulted on its debt and devalued its currency in 2001. The sell-off did not finally reach bottom until March of 2003.

During the first phase of this sell-off, the MSCI index of emerging markets plunged 58.6 percent from July 9, 1997, to September 10, 1998; rallied 124.8 percent by February 10, 2000; and then dropped another 53.7 percent by September 21, 2001.

In just the first downswing, the stock market in Indonesia lost almost all of its value, plunging 91.9 percent. Russian stocks plunged 87.2 percent, while the markets in Thailand, Malaysia, and Venezuela all lost just over three-quarters of their values.

Since this crisis, emerging market countries have moved up the credit-rating ladder as they have cleaned up their financial balance sheets, fought inflation, and built up cushions against adverse financial developments.

The International Monetary Fund (IMF) has cited the improvement in credit quality as a reason why "near-term risks to financial stability are declining" in emerging markets.[3] As of 2006, more than half of the 33 emerging market countries given credit ratings by Standard & Poor's were at an investment-grade level.

The overall credit rating of the bonds of the 32 countries in JPMorgan's EMBI Global index for emerging markets was up to BB+ at the end of 2006, its highest rating ever and just one notch below the lowest investment-grade credit rating. Among those countries on the current investment-grade list are Russia, which defaulted on its debt and devalued its currency in 1998, and Thailand, which set off the plunge in emerging markets in 1997. Mexico, which triggered the first broad emerging market debt crisis in the 1980s, is also investment grade now.

Another factor that has made emerging markets a little safer is that market contagion seems to have been significantly reduced. In years past, if one emerging market country, such as Thailand, had a problem, most of the other emerging countries suffered from the fallout.

One of the reasons for this decline in contagion is that emerging market countries have been modernizing their economies and have worked to avoid the debt problems that had sunk them in the past. In addition, investors have become better at distinguishing between one country and another.

In its September 2006 *Global Financial Stability Report* the IMF noted the 2006 emerging market sell-off, calling it a correction, and then asked what it said about the future:

> The correction raises the question: How resilient are emerging markets to future financial volatility? One lesson is that policy efforts across EMs have brought greater overall resilience against external shocks. Over time, country policy efforts have resulted in a migration of many EM sovereigns toward the safer end of the risk spectrum as measured by a variety of risk indicators.[4]

The IMF has also noted that a shift toward a longer-term view among institutional money managers in the developed countries is helping emerging market stability.

Noting that crises in the past were due, in part, to abrupt changes in capital flows, often by investors with only a short-term view, the IMF said that "based on current trends, global financial markets may very well be on track to be more and more dominated by such investors with a long-term view."[5]

At the same time, confidence has been growing that new emerging market country leaders would continue the same positive economic policies of their predecessors, even if the rhetoric of their political campaigns would make investors think differently. Luiz Inacio Lula da Silva, the leader of Brazil's left-wing Workers Party, was such a case. After he was inaugurated as president of Brazil at the beginning of 2003, it did not take long for investors to dispel their worries over whether he would continue current policies.

The confidence-building transition to President da Silva coincided with the beginning of the big rebound in emerging markets that overall saw the MSCI emerging market index finally eclipse its previous high, reached in 1993.

In the four years beginning in 2003, as can be seen in Figure 8.2, all the countries in the MSCI emerging market index outperformed the United States, some by a wide margin. The best-performing emerging markets were Egypt, up 1,056 percent; Colombia, up 705 percent; Argentina, up 556 percent; Brazil, up 458 percent; and the Czech Republic, up 406 percent. No emerging markets were down.

As these returns show, often it is the small markets (e.g., Egypt and Colombia) that suddenly surge, in part because their stocks are easily moved by a sudden buying spree by local investors or by hot money coming from abroad.

These small markets are not likely to be in any retail investor's personal portfolio or to be a big holding of a mutual fund investing across emerging markets. So it is the bigger, well-known emerging markets that will have more influence on your returns if you buy your exposure through mutual funds.

Another story of caution behind the new highs for emerging markets is that a rising tide does not always lift all boats. In Latin

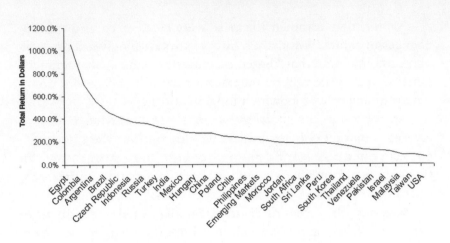

FIGURE 8.2   Wish You Were There

The returns from stocks in emerging markets for 2003 through 2006 have
outdone the U.S. stock market in every instance.
Source: MSCI.

American, where emerging markets were up 355 percent in the
four years through 2006, all but Venezuela reached new highs in
2006. But at the end of 2006, 8 of the 10 Asian emerging markets
were still below their record highs, all reached in the 1990s. Only
India and South Korea, two of the larger emerging stock markets,
had eclipsed their previous highs.

Emerging markets have also helped themselves with their
strong economic growth recently. In 2006, for example, the
economies of emerging countries, including many that have yet to
make it to official emerging market status in popular indexes, were
expected to grow at an annual rate of around 7 percent, according to the IMF, more than twice the pace of growth in the
world's developed economies.

Many of the obstacles to investing directly in stocks or bonds
in these countries have also been lowered or removed. These include capital controls, taxes, and fees. These markets are also
more open, with better accounting and disclosure requirements.

The banking systems in these countries, which are a sine qua
non for eventual graduation from emerging market status, are

also developing, although there is a lot more work to be done. The International Monetary Fund has offered some cautious praise, saying, "Banking systems in emerging markets have generally maintained their trend improvement. . . ."[6]

Emerging markets, including China, are also now the source of some of the biggest initial public offerings of stocks.

Of course, all of these positive developments, if they continue, mean that sometime in the years ahead the added risk that an investor picks up in these emerging markets is likely to decrease, which could also eventually lower the level of returns.

In fact, there were discussions among staff at the International Finance Corporation, where the name "emerging markets" was born, over whether it was still an appropriate tag for many of the countries it is describing.

"There is an interesting case to be made for calling them something else," acknowledged Joe O'Keefe, then the senior manager for corporate affairs at the IFC, in an interview during the IFC's 50th anniversary year. But the agency is sticking with "emerging markets" for now, he said.

Gary Kleiman, senior partner at Kleiman International Consultants in Washington, D.C., has been following emerging markets for 20 years and he thinks it might be time for a name change.

"The real emerging markets now are the next wave from Africa, Central Asia, Central America, and the Middle East," he said.

These next-up emerging markets are already in an index of 20 countries that Standard & Poor's calls Frontier Markets. They include: Bangladesh, Botswana, Bulgaria, Cote d'Ivoire, Croatia, Ecuador, Estonia, Ghana, Jamaica, Kenya, Latvia, Lebanon, Lithuania, Mauritius, Namibia, Romania, Slovenia, Trinidad and Tobago, Tunisia, and Ukraine.

So to this frontier is where some investors will have to go in the years ahead, especially if declining risk in the emerging markets also brings down their returns. But if you are thinking of going there now, we would offer the 10-to-15-year-old advice for what are still called emerging markets: You need a really strong stomach, do not put very much into your portfolio, and use only money that you can afford to lose.

FIXED INCOME

On the fixed-income side of emerging markets, change is afoot and that change is another sign of the emergence of emerging markets. The changes are likely, on the one hand, to open more opportunities to interested American investors and, on the other hand, to make some the choices more difficult. But these bond markets should continue to be a place to pick up some extra yield and to find some diversification for your portfolio.

Since the 1990s, the emerging bond market has been concentrated in Latin America and based on the so-called Brady bond, named for Nicholas F. Brady, the Treasury secretary in the George H.W. Bush administration. Denominated in dollars, Brady bonds were a key part of the solution to the debt crisis of the late 1980s. At the time, the Bush administration policy aimed to reduce the existing debt of troubled countries, like Mexico, Brazil, and Argentina, and, at the same time, provide them some new financing. Brady bonds worked and became the emerging market bond market.

While always on a rocky ride, like their sister stock markets, these bond markets were good performers overall in recent years, with a compound annual return of 10.9 percent, according to JP-Morgan, as they benefited from the same factors that have helped emerging stock markets, including the rise in credit ratings.

But the Brady bond market is drying up.

It is a casualty of the improved fortunes of emerging market countries, which have allowed them to pay off nearly all $150 billion of these bonds. And it is a casualty of the determination by some countries to break the link that tied them to financing from outside the country. Breaking this link makes these countries less vulnerable to external shocks, like those that precipitated past debt crises.

After Argentina defaulted on its bonds in 2001, other emerging market countries sought to further strengthen their bulwarks against external shocks by turning current account deficits to surpluses and by building up large stores of foreign currencies, especially dollars.

Mexico has paid off all its Brady bonds and done deals to swap other dollar-denominated debt for debt in pesos, its currency. Brazil has made substantial reductions in its short-term debt denominated in foreign currencies, is lowering barriers to foreigners in its local bond market, and has issued global bonds denominated in the real, its currency. Colombia, Venezuela (all of its Brady bonds), and Turkey also have reduced their external foreign-currency debt. Outstanding Brady bonds have declined from a high of $150 billion in 1996, based on the face value, to $10 billion in 2006, according to the IMF.[7]

What is developing in place of the Brady bond market are local markets where governments are raising the financing they need in their own currencies and corporations are beginning to sell their own private bonds.

"It appears that there has been a significant increase in structural allocations to local debt markets in recent years," the IMF noted in its September 2006 *Global Financial Stability Report.* "Although only incomplete data exist on foreign investor flows into local bond markets, they seem to confirm encouraging evidence from investor surveys."[8]

The report noted that there had been significant increases in foreign holdings of local currency government bonds in Brazil, Colombia, Mexico, Poland, and Turkey. The report also said that inflows from abroad helped offset the flight by speculative investors during the emerging market sell-off in 2006.

Another sign of the change in these markets is that in 2005 the total issuance of new debt by private corporations in emerging markets exceeded the issuance by governments for the first time.

There is also a growing interest from abroad in these emerging bond markets from Americans who also like the high-yield, junk bond market in the United States. In 2005 and 2006, net inflows into emerging market bond mutual funds was $2.5 billion, despite the outflows during 2006's midyear sell-off and well above the net inflow of $1.3 billion for the 10 years from 1992 through 2001, according to AMG Data Services. McCulley is putting 15 percent of his son's trust fund into these bond markets.

If this trend continues, which we expect, it will mean that Americans investing in these local bond markets will be taking on an additional risk—currency. Until now, the major portion of emerging market bonds that found their way into the hands of American investors, either directly or through mutual funds, were denominated in dollars, which meant there was no currency risk.

We cannot leave emerging markets without flagging, once again, that they are still a place for long-term investments, especially in stocks, and that the appetite for risk, which is fuel for these markets, can change quickly. And the recent behavior of some governments, like those of Venezuela and Bolivia, is running against the trend that brought on the improvement in these markets in the last decade. In other words, you are taking on more risk, so do not forget what that means.

Much of the sell-off in 2006 was a result of a pullback by investors who were suddenly worried about the risk they were taking. The rebound shows that some of those fears have diminished.

But with the economic slowdown in the United States at the end of 2006 and the possibility of one in the rest of the developed world, the risks for emerging markets could be rising again. Historically, they have not done well during a global slowdown. And a recession would be even worse, which is another reason why an economic downturn is a threat to investors.

And as usual some countries are better positioned to withstand trouble ahead than others. Those emerging markets still with big current account deficits, which mean they are far more dependent on money from abroad than other emerging market countries, are vulnerable. The IMF noted in the September 2006 *Global Financial Stability Report* that several emerging market countries, including Hungary, Slovakia, and Turkey, had large current account deficits that could pose a problem if the global climate sours. If that happened, the inflow of private foreign capital could slow dramatically. "In such a case, EM countries with large current account deficits would likely face a sharper adjustment path than currently envisaged," the report said.[9]

Investors who are worried about taking on this much risk can look to foreign developed markets, like the United Kingdom, Germany, France, Finland, Sweden, Italy, and Australia. More than half the world's stock market capitalization is outside of the United States, and of this, 85.2 percent is in the world's 22 developed markets, including Canada, outside of the United States. It is not a place you can afford to ignore completely. There are just too many stocks—and, therefore, opportunities—to choose from.

As noted in Chapter 1, investors can get a little better return, based on historical data, for only a little more risk in these markets, compared to the risk and return for the Standard & Poor's 500 stock index. These stock and bond markets are also safer than emerging markets. They are better regulated and have better laws protecting investors, more stable governments, and less market volatility than emerging markets.

They also have a lot of stocks that are well known to Americans, including automobile companies, electronics manufacturers, telephone companies, drug makers, and food companies. So they are much less of a mystery. And because they are outside of the United States, they do offer the added attraction of a bet on the weakening dollar.

CURRENCIES

That is the thing to remember about investing abroad—you are taking on a second risk: Besides buying foreign stocks or bonds, you are buying securities denominated in another currency, and this gives your international portfolio a second moving part.

At home, investors only have to calculate the gain or loss on the domestic, or American, stocks and bonds they have in their portfolios. With foreign stocks and bonds, they have to calculate the gain or loss on foreign securities and the gain or loss on the dollar versus the currency that the foreign stocks and bonds are denominated in.

When the proceeds from the sale of foreign securities are translated back into dollars, they shrink if the dollar has risen in value between the purchase and sale because the proceeds buy fewer dollars. If the dollar has fallen in value, the foreign currency proceeds would buy more dollars. So if the dollar rises in value, it reduces your return or increases your loss from abroad; if the dollar falls in value, it increases your return or reduces your loss from abroad.

For example, let's assume that you have 10 shares of a foreign stock traded in euro in your international portfolio. You bought it for 100 euro, when 1 euro was equal to $1.25, and a year later the stock was worth 110 euro. So the total return, assuming there is no dividend, is 10 percent, in euro. But if the dollar had risen 2 percent against the euro that year, so 1 euro was now worth $1.225, the total return would have dropped to 7.8 percent. Conversely, if the dollar fell 2 percent in value against the euro that year, with 1 euro now buying $1.276, the total return would rise to 12.2 percent.

You can calculate this easily for a stock or a stock index. Take the price of the stock or the level of a stock index at the beginning of the period and at the end of the period for which you want to calculate a return. Divide those figures by the number of foreign currency units to the dollar at the beginning of the period and at the end of the period. (Most currencies, such as the Japanese yen, the Swiss franc, and the Mexican peso, are quoted as the number of foreign units to the dollar. The euro, the British pound, and the Australian dollar are quoted in reverse—that is, the number of dollars to the euro, pound, and Australian dollar. In these cases, first divide the number of dollars per euro, pound, or Australian dollar into 1 to get the number of foreign currency units per dollar.) Then calculate the percentage change between the two and you have the return in dollars. Do the percentage change for the same stock or index in its local currency value and you can see the impact of the dollar on your investment.

From year to year, the dollar can make a big difference in the performance of the international portion of your portfolio. The recent dollar weakness is one big reason why American investors have been moving more money into foreign markets. Over long periods of time, since the dollar came off the gold standard and began to be freely traded in the 1970s, the trends are quite distinct, although they vary from currency to currency.

The dollar has been in a long-term decline against the Japanese yen and German mark, the leading currency in Europe before the euro. (It is still not known whether the dollar's long-term decline will continue with the euro, but we are betting on more decline in the next several years.)

But over time, the dollar has been rising against the British pound and was climbing against the French franc before it was replaced by the euro.

From the beginning of 1974 through the end of 2006, Japanese stocks had a total return of 1,966 percent, in dollar terms, as can be seen in Table 8.1, based on the MSCI index for Japanese stocks, including dividends. But most of that return was thanks to the decline in the value of the dollar, which dropped by more than half in this period. If the dollar had been unchanged, the return from Japanese stocks would have been 779 percent.

The return from German stocks was 3,780 percent, in dollar terms, up from 2,030 percent, in marks and euro, thanks to a decline in the dollar of almost 45 percent.

But the 18.7 percent rise in the value of the dollar against the British pound reduced returns for American investors from British stocks during the same period. In pounds, British stocks had a return of 6,032 percent, but in dollars that return fell to 5,072 percent, according to MSCI data. In France, the local currency return of 4,303 percent was shaved to 4,223 percent during this 33-year period.

But that erosion has not been as bad for investors as you might think, because even on a dollar basis the reduced returns

TABLE 8.1 How the Dollar Changed Returns from
Abroad, 1974–2006

	Dollars	Local Currency
Hurt by the Dollar		
Sweden	11,989%	17,971%
Hong Kong	7,603%	11,685%
United Kingdom	5,072%	6,032%
France	4,223%	4,303%
Australia	2,734%	5,258%
Canada	2,127%	2,491%
Norway	1,916%	2,094%
Spain	1,556%	3,552%
Italy	1,370%	3,408%
Helped by the Dollar		
Netherlands	8,022%	4,700%
Belgium	5,340%	3,927%
Switzerland	5,172%	1,881%
Denmark	4,938%	4,435%
Germany	3,780%	2,030%
Austria	3,273%	1,678%
World ex-U.S.	3,144%	2,039%
Singapore	2,100%	1,280%
Japan	1,966%	779%
United States	2,699%	2,699%

Total return for the period, in dollars and in local currency.
Source: MSCI.

were better than those available at home, except when compared
to Japan. (Both dollar returns from the United Kingdom and
France beat the 2,699 percent total return for American stocks,
based on the MSCI index for the United States.)

The same was true in emerging markets. From 1987 through
2006, the return, without dividends, from emerging markets was
812.7 percent, in dollar terms, which beats the 482.5 percent re-

turn from American stocks. But the rising dollar, or, more appropriately, plummeting emerging market currencies, did have an enormous impact. The local currency gain was off the charts, at 39,421 percent.

But as emerging markets move up the credit quality scale and improve their financial infrastructures, their currencies are going to be less vulnerable to the dollar, meaning the dollar could have less of a negative impact on these foreign returns over time.

So, if you are in for the longer term, a lot may depend on where you are making your bets. And there still are enough year-to-year swings to make a significant difference, up and down, over shorter periods, which is why you want to keep your eye on the value of the dollar when investing abroad. That way you have a chance to jump on and off a dollar trend at close to the right times.

Of course, instead of exposing yourself to the added risk of playing dollar moves, you can try to insulate yourself against the adverse swings—when the dollar is rising in value—by hedging. But we are advising against hedging until it is clear the dollar is rising again.

Hedging can lock in the future value of the dollar against a foreign currency by using futures contracts or other so-called derivatives. The problem for most Main Street investors is that this a difficult—and expensive—thing for an individual to do. It is better to search out a mutual fund or a money manager experienced in hedging. And remember, if you choose a fund that hedges and the dollar falls in value, you will not get the benefit of the dollar decline and you will have to bear the cost—in the fund's expenses—of hedging. That is why a lot of fund managers do not hedge. They think they are paid to pick stocks, not currencies.

AT HOME

The choices to increase your risk include small-cap stocks, corporate bonds, either investment-grade bonds or the non-investment-grade, high-yield bonds, and commodities.

Buying smaller-company or small-capitalization stocks is a little like buying emerging market stocks, although it is easier to do. Because these are newer companies and they are followed by fewer analysts on Wall Street, there is less information about them.

Investing in this sector (and taking on the added risk it brings) has paid off handsomely in recent years, especially considering that owning the stocks in the Standard & Poor's 500 stock index and the Dow Jones Industrial Average has not.

The compound annual return for the Russell 2000 Index of smaller-company stocks was 21.2 percent from 2003 through 2006, compared to 14.7 percent for the S&P 500 index. And while the Russell lagged the S&P 500 when it was rallying at the end of the 1990s, it did not suffer as much after the stock market bubble burst, which is another reason for adding small-cap stocks to a portfolio: They can help diversify.

Small-cap stocks are also a place where good money managers can find what McCulley calls ten-baggers, the stocks that can give you the big gains.

Both investment-grade corporate bonds and high-yield junk bonds are often recommended when interest rates are low or when the fixed-income market is in a decline, with prices falling and yields rising. If this is the case, the higher yields on investment-grade and high-yield bonds will help offset some of the capital losses as bond prices fall. We think that over the longer term they are just better than parking too much of your money in Treasuries.

An important thing to remember about junk bonds is that they have two distinct personalities, so their prices can be moved by one of those personalities on one day and by the other personality on another day. One is the personality of a bond and the other is the personality of a stock. Because of these two personalities, it is possible that a small downdraft in the stock market will not be as tough on junk bonds as one might think, as long as interest rates are coming down at the same time.

As for commodities, they are a wonderful crapshoot, and they also tell us a lot about the state of the economy. It used to be that this was the U.S. economy. But now commodities tell us more about demand in the global economy, as China's demand for oil and copper are big reasons why these prices soared in the beginning of the new century. In other words, if the global economy does slow down, commodity prices are going to slump. The slump in commodity prices in 2006 was making this sector look more attractive because prices had risen so much. And remember, as was shown in Chapter 2, commodities are good as a diversifier in your portfolio, helping to smooth out returns over time.

GETTING THERE

Buying abroad, particularly in emerging markets, still takes special expertise to make stock or bond picks and to actually buy them. In addition, there is less information available here on these markets and the stocks and bonds sold in them.

So it is going to be easier for most investors to get access to emerging market stocks and bonds through mutual funds if you want some picking by a portfolio manager. Or if actively managed funds are not your thing, there are index funds, which, like their name says, just invest in an existing index; for emerging market stocks this can be a leading index in a country, a region, or the whole emerging market universe.

Of course, buying mutual funds is not as simple as it sounds and requires, among other things, that a careful investor check out the performance history over time and be sure that, if it is an actively managed fund, the portfolio manager who did well in the past has not been suddenly replaced. It is also wise to know how diverse your exposure actually is in a particular emerging market fund. Some funds may have most of their money in a few stocks or in a few countries, even if the fund can invest anywhere in the emerging market universe.

And checking on the costs of your fund is always important. Across the board, from mutual funds to exchange-traded funds

(ETFs), you have to be cost conscious, since your returns are actually what you make minus what you pay to get them.

If an American investor wants to go it alone, there are many ways to do it. American depositary receipts (ADRs) are available for stocks from emerging markets. The depositary receipt allows American investors to buy the shares of the underlying foreign stock in dollar terms in the United States and watch them trade on an exchange or in the over-the-counter market. But depositary receipts do not eliminate the currency risk because moves in the price of the underlying foreign stock and the value of the dollar against the stock's home currency combine to change the dollar price of the depositary receipt. And investors have to decide which emerging market stocks to buy for their portfolio and how much of each one.

One way to make this decision is to follow the weighting used by mutual funds that are investing abroad in emerging markets—and doing well. But beware that the data available on mutual fund company web sites or at Morningstar (www.morningstar.com), which tracks mutual fund performance, may not be current.

Another route for individual investors are ETFs, which are coming on strong because they are easy for investors to buy and can put broad exposure to various markets into a portfolio quickly. For emerging markets, they are based on indexes of countries, regions, and the entire asset class. They are often cheaper than an index mutual fund and can be traded on exchanges all day, like stocks, so investors can get in and out in a hurry (but still have to pay a commission, just as they would on a stock, and still have the same foreign currency exposure they would have with ADRs or in an unhedged international mutual fund). ETFs also provide immediate diversification because you are buying an index that covers a country or a region or the whole emerging market universe.

But no matter how the decisions are made, investors have to remember that you do not want to overconcentrate your emerging market investments in just a few stocks or countries. So an index of emerging markets through a mutual fund or an ETF is an attractive route to take.

McCulley is putting 35 percent of his son's trust fund into emerging market stocks, using a combination of index and actively managed mutual funds. We are not advocating that much for everyone. But you should consider emerging markets for a good third to a half of your foreign stock exposure, which itself should be closer to 50 percent than 25 percent of the entire stock allocation.

Buying foreign stocks in developed markets is much easier. There are many more ADRs for foreign stocks from developed markets and a much broader selection of indexed mutual funds and ETFs for foreign developed markets, regions, and sectors, like energy, technology, health care, and industrials. Small-cap stocks are also easy to buy, but investors who are venturing into this area for the first time to pick up more risk probably should do this through a mutual fund or an index fund. If it is an actively managed mutual fund, you want to go for one that has a good long-term reputation and track record in small-cap stocks, not just a fund that had been hot in the past 12 months. Consistency over time is what produces the good returns—the ten-baggers.

Both investment-grade corporate bonds and high-yield junk bonds are best added to your portfolio through a mutual fund, again because the picking is difficult. When buying junk bonds through a mutual fund, also remember that you may not get the return you think you will if you are looking at the performance of an index, like the Lehman Brothers index of junk bonds. This is because the index includes many lower-rated junk bonds that a lot of mutual funds are unwilling, or are not allowed, to own. So if there is a big rally in the market, these lower-rated bonds will add to the return of the index but will not be doing that for a mutual fund that does not own them.

If a large portion of the junk bonds in a mutual fund portfolio have credit ratings near investment grade, you may not be getting the extra amount of risk you desire.

Commodities can be bought in many ways, including through ETFs, either on commodity indexes or on individual commodities, including gold.

And, finally, if you are going to keep some Treasury securities in your portfolio, consider buying them yourself, rather than through a mutual fund that specializes in them. The reason is simple: You can protect yourself against some unwanted losses.

If you buy Treasuries through a mutual fund and interest rates start to rise, the fund is likely to sell some of the Treasury securities it is holding so it can buy securities with higher yields as interest rates rise. That raises the yield it can advertise. But the fund will be taking capital losses as it is doing this, because Treasury prices fall as yields rise.

If you buy your Treasury securities yourself, you can avoid these capital losses by just holding the securities to maturity. If you do this, think about when you might need the money that goes into Treasury securities, so that you can buy maturities that you can afford to hold until they mature.

It is very easy now to buy Treasury securities yourself, with no broker or commission involved. Just go to the Treasury Direct web site (www.treasurydirect.gov) and follow directions. The purchases are paid for by direct debt to your bank account.

BONDS AND THE FED

One of the differences between bond portfolios and stock portfolios is that there are more reasons to make regular adjustments in your bond portfolio than to your stock portfolio. This is because changes in the interest rate cycle from rising to falling, or falling to rising, can make a difference in both the return and the risk of your bond portfolio.

This is not to say that there are no reasons to be defensive in the stock market, even if you are a long-term investor, or that you should not get out of your clear equity losers and put the money elsewhere. But remember that you play in the stock market to win, while in the bond market you play not to lose.

The manufacturing index (the Purchasing Managers' Index or PMI) released each month by the Institute for Supply Management, which is McCulley's favorite indicator, can be used by investors as a guide to when to switch their interest rate bets.

Bond bear markets tend to reach their nadir when the PMI is peaking, usually around 60. The peak is a reflection of a strong economy and the threat of inflation that comes with that. So before the peak in the PMI, the Fed has been raising interest rates to curb growth and inflation. The average of PMI peaks since 1982 is 60.7. The highest peak was 69.9 in December 1983.

Likewise, the best of the bull bond market tends to be about over once the PMI has bottomed, usually around 45, because the Fed is near or at the end of cutting interest rates to reverse the economic slowdown that pulled the PMI lower. The average of PMI troughs since 1982 is 44.3. The lowest trough was 39.2 in January 1991.

Even if the Fed keeps tightening after the peak or easing after the trough, the bond market will see what is going on with the PMI and anticipate what that means for the future of the Fed's current monetary policy—either ending the tightening or stopping the easing—and move before the Fed does. So bonds often start a new bull market in the final throes of Fed tightening and a new bear market in the final throes of Fed easing.

Investors can anticipate, too. If their money is in a bond mutual fund, investors can move it back and forth between a fund with high duration and one with low duration—in other words, from a bond fund filled with longer-term securities to a bond fund filled with short-term securities.

Let's just stop here for a quick recap of the definition of duration, which was done in more detail in Chapter 6. Duration is a measure of a bond's, or a portfolio's, sensitivity to a move in interest rates. The longer the duration, the bigger the move in the price of the bond when interest rates move up or down.

So when the PMI is peaking, a forecast of a coming decline in interest rates, you would want your bond money in a long-duration fund because the prices of its longer-term bonds will move up the most with the decline in interest rates, adding capital gains to your total return. When the PMI is bottoming, a forecast

One of the confusing things about bonds for many investors is that their prices and yields move in opposite directions. Here is why.

Let's start with a $1,000 bond with a coupon of 5 percent.

The coupon is the interest paid annually, usually in two semiannual payments, on the face, or par, value of the bond. But when a bond trades, its price—that $1,000—can move up and down. If the price an investor pays for the bond is more than $1,000, the 5 percent interest is still paid just on the $1,000 face value of the bond. So the yield on the price paid for the bond, let's say $1,002, is actually less than 5 percent.

The reverse is true if the price paid for the bond is below $1,000. The 5 percent is still paid on the $1,000, but the investor, let us say, paid just $998 for the bond; so the resulting yield on what was actually paid for the bond is more than 5 percent. Thus when the prices of bonds fall, the yields rise; and when the prices of bonds rise, the yields fall. When new issues of bonds are sold they are usually priced just below the face value so that the yield is slightly higher than the coupon on the bond.

Your annual total return consists of the interest rate paid and whatever loss or gain there is in the move in the bond price.

of a coming rise in interest rates, you switch to the short-duration fund, because the prices of its shorter-term bonds move less when rates rise, so the capital loss is mitigated.

Doing this switch from January 1991 to August 2006 produced a compound annual rate of return of 6.9 percent, according to the financial engineers at PIMCO. Staying put in a short-duration fund produced a compound annual return of 5.4 percent. And staying put in a long-duration fund produced an annual return of 7 percent.

Wait. Staying put with long duration produced a higher return than switching from longer-term bonds to shorter-term bonds. Yes, it did, but with much higher risk. The standard deviation of staying put in long duration was 3.8 compared to 2.7 for the duration-switching strategy.

So what do you do? We will use the Sharpe ratio again, as we did in Chapter 2, to evaluate the risk and reward of these two investment strategies. The Sharpe ratio tells you which portfolio is giving you the better return for the risk taken.

In the duration switching case, after subtracting the risk-free rate from the average rate of return and dividing by the standard deviation of the risk-free rate over the same period, the Sharpe ratio comes out at 1.06. The Sharpe ratio for staying put in long duration is 0.80. So duration switching is a better strategy for the risk taken, and the difference in return is not big.

But if you do not want to embark on this kind of switching strategy, the Sharpe ratio tells you that the short-duration strategy, with a ratio of 0.87, is more attractive than the long-duration strategy, with its 0.80 ratio. But in a world where you have to get higher returns to stay even, that choice is not a good one because the difference in returns (7.0 for long duration versus 5.4 for short duration) is too large. As we said in Chapter 2, investors should first determine the higher return they need and then use the Sharpe ratio to help them pick strategies that provide them with that return. But investors should not be ruled by the Sharpe ratio. Your broker, money manager, or anyone who is helping you with your investing should be able to provide Sharpe ratios for you.

The fact that an investor can get a slightly better return by just staying put in the long-duration fund does stand conventional wisdom on its head a bit, since it naturally appears that you want to have shorter duration, or maturities, in your portfolio when interest rates are rising and longer duration when interest rates are coming down. That is what happens in investing and why hard-and-fast rules are not a good idea.

Of course, there are many more instances in which this conventional wisdom does work. But this exception to the rule shows that investors always have to consider the risk-return trade-off.

And as we have said, to get the higher returns needed in the future there are times when investors will just have to grin and bear it.

Here is one more tidbit on betting on bonds. Going against the grain can be as important in the bond market as it is in stocks. As long as the Fed maintains its credibility as an inflation fighter, investors will have to remember to be contrarian when they are thinking about inflation. This means that they should bet that interest rates will fall when inflationary fears push interest rates higher, and vice versa. That way they are anticipating, which means they can make more money.

STOCKS AND THE FED

Now let's look at the performance of equities when the Federal Reserve is in a tightening cycle and see how bad this is for your stock portfolio.

While we cannot depend on history to repeat itself, stocks have done a lot better than investors might think when the Fed has been raising interest rates in the past, as can be seen in Table 8.2. One of the reasons for this may be that as the Fed has gained credibility as an inflation fighter over the past two decades, a tightening cycle is seen more as a move to keep inflation in check, rather than a desperate effort to tame inflation after it has gotten out of hand. In the past, when inflation got out of hand, it was a big knock on future corporate earnings and undermined the stock market. So confidence in the Fed, if it is maintained by the central bank's policy makers, can save investors money.

In the tightening cycle that ran from June of 2004 to June of 2006 (there were no further rate increases in 2006) the Standard & Poor's 500 stock index rose 14.1 percent from the month before the first rate increase by the Fed on June 30, 2004, to a month after the last rate increase.

There were only two stock market declines from the start to the finish of the eight Fed tightenings since 1971, and only one

TABLE 8.2   What Happens to Stocks When the Fed Tightens?

Period 1		
Start	2/1/1971	
End	8/15/1974	−20.9%
Period 2		
Start	10/26/1976	
End	3/28/1980	−0.4%
Period 3		
Start	7/7/1980	
End	6/25/1981	12.3%
Period 4		
Start	4/25/1983	
End	9/25/1984	4.3%
Period 5		
Start	11/25/1986	
End	3/23/1989	16.4%
Period 6		
Start	1/4/1994	
End	3/1/1995	4.0%
Period 7		
Start	6/1/1999	
End	6/16/2000	13.2%
Period 8		
Start	5/28/2004	
End	7/28/2006	14.1%

Percent change in the S&P 500 index from one month before the Fed began raising interest rates to one month after it stopped.
Source: Federal Reserve, Standard & Poor's.

was significant, the 20.9 percent plunge in the S&P 500 index from February 1971 to the middle of August 1974. The other decline, of just 0.4 percent, was from January 1976 to March 1980. Both those performances came around the deep recession of the mid-1970s and a bout of stagflation, with both unemployment and inflation on the rise at the same time. And while the Fed had begun its fight against inflation in 1979, it had not yet won its credibility in the financial markets, even though that opening volley saw the Fed's target for short-term interest rates hit 20 percent in 1980 and again in 1981. Since then, all the tightening cycles have come as the Fed was building toward its victory over inflation.

In all eight of the cycles since 1971, the average increase for the S&P 500 from a month before to a month after each cycle was 5.4 percent. The average of the increases was 10.7 percent, with the biggest a 16.4 percent run from November 1986 to March 1989. That tightening cycle included a pause after the stock market crash of 1987, when the Fed cut rates. But policy makers started raising rates again in the spring of 1988. The smallest rally of the Fed's interest rate raising cycles was 4 percent from February 1994 to March 1995. That was when the Fed raised its fed funds rate by three percentage points in 12 months.

For long-term investors, even the average performance is of the kind that should make you less worried about sticking with stocks through a Fed tightening cycle. And, as we mentioned in Chapter 4, this performance could be a reason to move money from bonds into stocks even when interest rates are rising.

Obviously, when interest rates are about to fall is the best time to move money from bonds to stocks. Equities have performed much better when the Fed is easing, or cutting interest rates, except in the most recent cycle. From December 2000 to July 2003, the S&P 500 was down 24.6 percent. But without the Fed pushing its benchmark short-term interest rate down to 1 percent from 6.5 percent, the stock market would not have had the big rebound that began in March of 2003. By the end of the year, the S&P 500 had jumped 26.4 percent for the year, with a total return, with dividends, of 28.7 percent.

In the six other easing cycles since 1971, all the rallies were double-digit, producing an average of 41.5 percent. From June 1995 to December 1998, the beginning of the stock market bubble and the big bull run of the second half of the 1990s, the stock market was up 121.3 percent.

WHAT ABOUT CHINA?

The dominant force on interest rates on a one-to-two-year horizon is the pace of economic growth. But China's transition away from its currency tie to the dollar could have a significant impact on the margin. That impact would be even larger if the transition is quick or disorderly.

If the U.S. economy were going into a recession, interest rates would be going down here anyway, no matter what China did. But they would go down less because China would have billions fewer dollars to recycle into the U.S. bond market as it allowed its currency, the yuan, to rise in value against the dollar.

This fact could complicate the Fed's effort to restart the economy, possibly forcing the policy makers to push their short-term interest rate target lower than anticipated. The added inflationary pressure arising from China's unwinding of its currency tie, which would make its exports to the United States more expensive, could also get in the way of the Fed. The threat of inflation could retard the fall of longer-term interest rates, undermining the Fed's effort to encourage business investment and revive the housing market.

Such a situation would be the reverse of what happened when the Fed started raising interest rates in June 2004 to slow growth and curb inflation. Longer-term interest rates did not rise at all in the beginning (in part because of China's tie of the yuan to the dollar), which kept the housing market stronger longer and probably forced Fed policy makers to push their short-term interest rate target higher than they expected to get the economy to slow.

So the financial environment of a recession and China unwinding its tie to the dollar could be a time when a lot of mistakes could be made because what would normally be expected to happen would not.

In bond market jargon, a bet that long-term rates will come down less than short-term rates means that the yield curve will be steeper than expected. Bond portfolio managers would concentrate their money in the front, or short-term end, of the yield curve, getting the capital gains as prices of these securities rose as short-term interest rates fell. But they would put less money than usual in longer-term securities because China could make the yields on 10-year notes and 30-year bonds very sticky on the way down. A fall of the dollar, which would come with the untying of the yuan link, could kill the appetite of private foreign investors for dollar-denominated paper, undermining stocks and also impeding the decline in interest rates.

In this case, investors with money in bond mutual funds would again have to make an adjustment in the conventional wisdom. Since longer-term rates would come down less than shorter-term rates, investors would not want to put nearly as much money into longer-term securities as they would if interest rates were coming down across the yield curve. Instead of shifting your money to a long-duration fund, you would keep much of it in a short-duration fund, where it probably was if the Fed was raising interest rates before the recession.

For stock portfolios, this scenario could mean a longer wait for a revival of earnings growth. But it would not be a good reason to alter your long-term route in one direction or another.

If China's transition process is deliberate and orderly, there is less to do, assuming the economy here is growing moderately. That would put the economy, and most likely the Fed, on a straightaway as higher than otherwise interest rates helped offset some of the additional inflationary pressure. So there is not a lot that can be done in a portfolio of bonds or stocks.

TIPS AND DEFLATION

Treasury Inflation Protected Securities, or TIPS, would not seem all that useful in a time when the Fed has won the battle for price stability. But they could turn out to be a good hedge.

As we noted in the discussion of recessions in Chapter 3, Bill Gross of PIMCO believes that the Fed will have to prime the pump too much to get the economy out of its next slump. He argues that this pump priming will push prices above their stable level, which is between 2 percent and 3 percent inflation. If that happens, then TIPS would be a nice addition to a portfolio, because investors would be compensated for the rise in inflation with an increase in the principal, or face value, of their TIPS.

So if you feel this way, TIPS should be slipped into the fixed-income portion of your portfolio, no matter how small it may be. McCulley has 25 percent of his portfolio for the Morgan le Fay Dreams Foundation in TIPS for just this reason. And because TIPS have a very low correlation with stocks, they are a good diversifier in your portfolio.

And now let's turn our attention to deflation. The first thing to do in the face of a deflation threat is to remember that deflation is highly unlikely to actually happen. The Fed has both the ability and the will to prevent it. But that does not mean that financial markets will not trade on that threat for a while, even if it is unlikely to be realized.

During that period of market fright, long-duration Treasury securities would have their day in the sun, soaring in price in anticipation of big declines in short-term rates as the Fed eases as part of its antideflation campaign. Risky assets, including those in emerging markets and bonds with lower credit ratings, will not do well.

But if you believe, as we do, that any deflation threat would be thwarted, the right thing to do is to enjoy the positive ride on what Treasuries you do have. It will be a minitrend. As interest rates fall here, buying stocks and bonds abroad as a bet against the dollar would also be profitable. And when the deflation threat has passed, swap some of the winners—the Treasury securities—for what were the losers—lower-rated bonds and emerging market stocks.

RECESSION

A recession means that interest rates are going to be pushed very low by the Fed, and maybe very quickly. Therefore, there is another big bull market for bonds in the offing. This is what happened around the last recession, which ran from March to November of 2001. From 2000 through 2002, the bond market had three really good years, with a compound annual rate of return of 10.1 percent, according to Lehman Brothers. Because Fed policy makers would be worried about deflation in the next recession, they can be expected to be clear that they will push rates as low as they have to go for as long as necessary. The bond market would respond nicely to such a commitment. The central bank's short-term interest rate target got to 1 percent in the wake of the most recent recession. It could go lower in the next one.

So moving some money from stocks, especially those that have performed poorly, is a good idea, as long as you are prepared to move it back into equities as the economy turns around.

In judging how low interest rates will go, investors will want to know how much of the burden for reviving the economy will fall on the Fed. The government could help a lot by cutting taxes and increasing spending. That would enlarge the budget deficit and administer a big dose of old-fashioned Keynesian medicine that would stimulate the economy. But if the White House and the Congress were suddenly worried about bigger budget deficits and therefore did very little, the entire job of economic revival would be left to the Fed. And that means short-term interest rates could go to zero. In addition, the Fed might have to employ other strategies to get interest rates low enough to spur growth, like bringing down longer-term interest rates by stepping into the Treasury market and buying the Treasury's 10-year notes.

So the decision to use or not to use deficit spending at the onset of a recession would make a difference in how far interest rates were likely to fall.

The drop in interest rates also would probably make the dollar weaker. This would be an added argument for sending money abroad to reap the currency gains as the dollar fell further. But if the recession here also means a slowdown in the rest of the world, that bet becomes less appealing because interest rates would be cut abroad to spur growth there, limiting the dollar's decline. Foreign bonds, however, would still look good because interest rates would be coming down abroad.

As for foreign stocks, the end of the recession could be a good time to add some to your portfolio if they have fallen along with U.S. stocks.

TRENDS

While investors need to be long-term generally, they can improve returns by trying to take advantage of trends in markets. This includes taking advantage of newborn bubbles.

Bubbles are not predictable, like hurricanes, because each bubble has its own idiosyncratic internal rhythm, similar to the frivolity in an Irish pub on Friday night. But in their infancy all bubbles are just trends. They are the straightaways of the investing world and need to be used to make money. The problem with this advice is that it sounds like market timing, and investing for the long term, especially in stocks, runs counter to market timing, which involves jumping on and off trends just at the right moment.

But there are times when trends become easily identifiable and it is still not too late to take advantage. This is especially true in the fixed-income market, because the Federal Reserve is more and more clear about which direction interest rates are moving in and for how long. Stock trends are also identifiable, like the recent up-and-down performance of big-cap stocks versus small-cap stocks. There are also broad trends that can be followed, like the lift that emerging stock markets will get over time because of the more rapid economic growth in these countries than in the developed economies of the United States, Japan, and Europe.

The weakness of the dollar is another such trend. We think that as long as the current account deficit is around record levels—and knowing that China will unravel its tie with the dollar one way or another—the U.S. currency is in a longer-term decline against the world's major currencies. The dollar may even weaken further against the currencies, like the British pound, that it has been rising against over the past four decades.

A look at the performance of the dollar and the euro will show how even an up-and-down performance of the dollar against foreign currencies can be beneficial for American investors. And that means a longer-term decline of the dollar will be a really nice boost to returns for those who buy foreign stocks and bonds to add risk to their portfolios.

The euro, now the currency of 12 European nations in what some analysts call Euroland, made its debut on January 1, 1999. Its introduction, no matter how the dollar fared against it, greatly simplified the currency puzzle for American investors by eliminating a lot of other currencies to watch. With fewer moving parts, any portfolio is easier to manage.

Although the euro was expected to debut with a nice rally against the dollar, it fell, which was a big drag on the international portions of American portfolios. From the debut to the end of 2001, the MSCI index for stocks in the countries using the euro rose 12.4 percent in euro, including dividends. But when that gain was translated back into dollars, those stocks had a loss of 14.8 percent because the dollar's value had risen 31.9 percent against the euro.

Then from the end of 2001 to the end of 2004, the dollar plunged 34.5 percent against the euro and turned a 14.9 percent loss on Euroland stocks into a 29.9 percent gain in dollars. In that same time period, the total return for the S&P 500 index was 11.2 percent. So a 29.9 percent gain on foreign stocks that themselves went down really looks good. This is the kind of tonic portfolios like.

The dollar rallied some in the following two years through 2006, reducing a total return of 50.5 percent in stocks in Euroland to 46 percent in dollars. But, once again, even that reduced performance outdid the S&P 500, which retuned 21.5 percent. And over the entire period, from the beginning of 1999 through 2006, the return in euro was 43.9 percent, while the return in dollars was 61.6 percent. And the S&P 500 return was 30.9 percent. Playing the dollar was—and is—a good idea.

WHERE TO, PORTFOLIO?

So, if you take any of this advice, where is your portfolio going to go?

Here are two sample portfolios that should give you a picture of where you could be on the risk scale and where you can move to by making changes in your own portfolio. In calculating the historic returns and the risk measure, the standard deviation, we use the performance of indexes, like the S&P 500 and the Russell 2000 of small-cap stocks. For investing abroad, we use MSCI indexes. For fixed income we use the Lehman bond index.

Using indexes mean that the investments are broader (less concentrated) than might be made by an actively managed mutual fund or an individual investor. In that case, the risk might be a little understated, as well as the annualized returns.

But remember, this is historical data. It is in no way a promise of what will happen in the future. We use it because investors have to have some basis for making a choice.

The returns and risk levels will not compare to those used in Chapter 1. Both portfolios are diversified, which changes the returns and risks. In addition, the returns and the standard deviations for stocks go back no further than the 1970s because that is when Lehman Brothers began its indexes for the Treasury and overall fixed-income markets.

Our first sample portfolio consists of 60 percent stocks and 40 percent bonds, with all the stocks in the Standard & Poor's 500 stock index and all the bonds in the Treasury market.

The compound annual return of this portfolio is 10.9 percent, based on data back to 1974.[10] The risk, or standard deviation, is 9.8. This is conservative, especially for someone with 30 or 40 years to retirement, despite the nice-looking return. The return is high because the portfolio's history includes both the 1990s for stocks and the bull market in bonds as the Fed conquered inflation. (We could have started with an even more conservative portfolio, but we think you will get the point.)

The second portfolio is 95 percent stocks, with half of those abroad, roughly matching the global equity distribution. Half of the foreign stocks (23.75 percent of the portfolio) come from emerging markets, and the rest are from developed foreign markets. In the United States, the equity portion is split evenly between the S&P 500 and the Russell 2000 of small-cap stocks. The 5 percent of fixed income is split between the investment-grade corporate bond market and the high-yield junk bond market.

The compound annual return for this portfolio is 12 percent, with a risk level of 14.2, based on data going back to 1988.

So what is the difference? Using the Sharpe ratio, the 60/40 portfolio looks like a better trade-off between return and risk. But by the compounding of returns rule, the 95 percent stock portfolio, which takes on more risk to get a higher return, looks better. After 30 years the riskier portfolio is almost 34 percent larger. Starting with $100,000, that means an additional three quarters of a million dollars in the portfolio.

There are many other possible portfolio combinations. But you get the point. Add risk. Look abroad. If you are older, get into emerging markets, even if you keep some money in bonds. If you are young, think U.S. stocks, foreign stocks, and emerging market stocks, and then just read your financial statements twice a year. And, of course, keep adding to the portfolio.

If you are determined to remain conservative and at home—which you should not—at least spice up the equity and fixed-income portions of your portfolio.

So drive a little faster—and confidently—on the curves and straightaways ahcad.

Notes

Introduction

1. Congressional Budget Office, "Updated Long-Term Projections for Social Security," June 2006, 1 (www.cbo.gov/publications/collections/socialsecurity.cfm#pt2).
2. Portions of "Fed Focus" and "Global Central Bank Focus," © 1999–2006 Pacific Investment Management Company LLC, have been excerpted and used herein by license from, and with the permission of, PIMCO. PIMCO owns and retains all right, title, and interest in and to the "Fed Focus" and "Global Central Bank Focus" publications, which may not be copied, modified, or otherwise used without the express written consent of PIMCO.
3. All material in this book from *The New York Times* is copyright © The New York Times and all material from Times Books is copyright © Times Books.

Chapter 1   New Steps

1. The compound annual rate of return, or the compound annual growth rate, allows investors to compare the returns from different investments, even if they are over different time periods and even if the returns are up and down. A simple average will not work for this kind of comparison. In the calculation of the compound annual rate, the actual return for each year is added to—or subtracted from, in the case of a loss—the principal. The compound annual rate based on these calculations shows you what would have to have been earned each year of the investment time period to achieve the

cumulative return for that period. For example, the Standard & Poor's 500 stock index had a cumulative return of 138.5 percent from 1996 through 2005, including dividends. The actual annual returns were, by year, 23 percent, 33.4 percent, 28.6 percent, 21 percent, minus 9.1 percent, minus 11.9 percent, minus 22.1 percent, 28.7 percent, 10.9 percent, and 4.9 percent. The average return is 10.74 percent. But the compound annual rate of return is 9.08 percent—the return that would be needed each year to produce the cumulative return of 138.5 percent.

2. Mary Williams Walsh, "When Your Pension Is Frozen . . . ," *The New York Times*, January 22, 2006, Nation, www.nytimes.com, Copyright © 2006 The New York Times; Mary Williams Walsh, "Public Pension Plans Face Billions in Shortages," *The New York Times*, August 8, 2006, Business, www.nytimes.com, Copyright © 2006 The New York Times.

3. The data in this book on returns and standard deviations from Ibbotson Associates, a Morningstar company, is being used with the permission of Ibbotson Associates. The returns and standard deviations have been calculated by Ibbotson using their own data and data from the sources mentioned in the text.

4. Copyright © 2007 Lehman Brothers Inc. Used with permission. The Book is not sponsored, endorsed, sold or promoted by Lehman Brothers Inc. ("Lehman Brothers"). Lehman Brothers makes no representations or warranty, express or implied, to the authors, publisher and/or readers of the Book or any member of the public regarding the advisability of investing in any securities generally or the ability of the Lehman Index to track general bond market performance. Lehman Brothers' only relationship to the Licensee is the licensing of the Lehman Index which is determined, composed and calculated by Lehman Brothers without regard to the Licensee or the Book. Lehman Brothers has no obligation to take the needs of the Licensee or the authors, publishers and/or readers of the Book into consideration in determining, composing or calculating the Lehman Index. Lehman Brothers has no

obligation or liability in connection with the distribution and marketing of the Book.

Lehman Brothers does not guarantee the quality, accuracy and/or the completeness of the Lehman Index or any data included therein, or otherwise obtained by licensee, authors, publishers and/or readers of the Book, or any other person or entity from the use of the Lehman Index in connection with the rights licensed hereunder or for any other use. Lehman Brothers makes no express or implied warranties, and hereby expressly disclaims all warranties of merchantability of fitness for a particular purpose or use with respect to the Lehman Index or any data included therein. Without limiting any of the foregoing, in no event shall Lehman Brothers have any liability for any special punitive, indirect, or consequential damages (including lost profits), even if notified of the possibility of such damages.

5. All data in this book from Standard & Poor's is used with the permission of Standard & Poor's. Copyright © 2007 The McGraw-Hill Companies, Inc. Standard & Poor's, including its subsidiary corporations (S&P), is a division of the McGraw-Hill Companies, Inc. Reproduction of this data in any form is prohibited without S&P's prior permission.

6. All MSCI data in the book is used with the permission of MSCI. The MSCI data contained herein is the property of Morgan Stanley Capital International Inc. (MSCI). MSCI, its affiliates, and information providers make no warranties with respect to any such data. The MSCI data contained herein is used under license and may not be further used, distributed, or disseminated without the express written consent of MSCI.

7. All data from JPMorgan in this book is used with the permission of JPMorgan and is Copyright © 2007.

8. All data from Goldman Sachs used in this book is used with the permission of Goldman Sachs. All data Copyright © 2007 by Goldman Sachs.

9. International Monetary Fund, "Global Financial Stability Report, Aspects of Global Asset Allocation," September 2005, 87.

10. Investment Company Institute and Securities Industry Association, *Equity Ownership in America, 2005*, Chapter 2: "Equity Investors' Characteristics," 22, Figure 30 (www.ici.org/statements/res/rpt_05_equity_owners.pdf).

11. Ibid., 19, Figure 24.

12. All AMG data is used with the permission of AMG Data Services. Copyright © 2007 AMG Data Services—All Rights Reserved.

13. Hewitt Associates, "How Well Are Employees Saving and Investing in 401(k) Plans," *2006 Hewitt Universal Benchmarks*, 47.

14. Ibid., 4.

15. Hewitt Associates, "How Well Are Employees Saving and Investing in 401(k) Plans," *2005 Hewitt Universal Benchmarks*, 45.

CHAPTER 2   More Than Stocks, More Than Bonds

1. All data used in this book from Russell Investment Group is used with permission of Russell Investment Group and is Copyright © 2007.

2. International Monetary Fund, *Global Financial Stability Report*, Chapter 3: "Aspects of Global Asset Allocation," September 2005, 92.

3. Kirt C. Butler and Domingo C. Joaquin, "Are the Gains from International Portfolio Diversification Exaggerated? The Influence of Downside Risk in Bear Markets," July 9, 2001 (Presented at the European Financial Management Association [EFMA] 2002 London meetings). Available at Social Science Research Network (SSRN): http://ssrn.com/abstract=221992 or DOI: 10.2139/ssrn.221992.

4. Ibid.

5. Here is how to calculate a Sharpe ratio. In a spreadsheet, first put in the annual returns from the investments you want to analyze, such as the returns from a stock index in the United States and abroad. Then subtract what economists call the

risk-free rate for each year from these returns. This can be the annual return on a 30-day Treasury bill, which is the safest of investments. (You can find historical interest rate data at the Federal Reserve's web site at www.federalreserve.gov/releases/h15/data.htm.) What you get is called the excess return. Then you calculate the annual average (not the compound annual rate of return) of this excess return and the standard deviation of this excess return using the formulas for average and standard deviation in an Excel spreadsheet and divide the standard deviation into the annual average. The result is the Sharpe ratio. When you are comparing returns for individual investments or from portfolios, the higher the resulting Sharpe ratio, the more attractive the return is for the risk taken. But as we note, sometimes it might be better to choose the higher return.

6. Stefano Cavaglia, Jeffrey Diermeier, Vadim Moroz, and Sonia De Zordo, "Investing in Global Equities," *Journal of Portfolio Management* (Spring 2004); Stefano Cavaglia, Dimitris Melas, and George Tsouderos, "Cross-Industry and Cross-Country International Equity Diversification," *Journal of Investing* (Spring 2000).

CHAPTER 3   What Can Go Wrong

1. Timothy F. Geithner, "Policy Implications of Global Imbalances" (Speech, Global Financial Imbalances Conference, Chatham House, London, January 23, 2006) (www.ny.frb.org/newsevents/speeches/2006/gei060123.html).
2. Congressional Budget Office, "The Budget and Economic Outlook: An Update," August 2006, Summary Table 1, x. See the CBO web site for updates (www.cbo.gov/budget/budproj.shtml).
3. Congressional Budget Office, "Updated Long-Term Projections for Social Security," June 2006, 1. See the CBO web site for updates (www.cbo.gov/publications/collections/socialsecurity.cfm#pt2).

4. Congressional Budget Office, "The Budget and Economic Outlook: An Update," August 2006, Summary XI. See the CBO web site for updates (www.cbo.gov/budget/budproj.shtml).

5. Alan Greenspan, "Economic Flexibility" (Speech, National Association for Business Economics Annual Meeting, Chicago, Illinois [via satellite], September 27, 2005) (www.federalreserve.gov/boarddocs/speeches/2005/20050927/default.htm).

6. Alan Greenspan, "Semiannual Monetary Policy Report to the Congress" (Testimony, Committee on Financial Services, U.S. House of Representatives, July 20, 2005) (www.federalreserve.gov/boarddocs/hh/2005/july/testimony.htm).

7. Alan Greenspan, "Reflections on Central Banking" (Speech, Federal Reserve Bank of Kansas City, Jackson Hole, Wyoming, August 26, 2005) (www.federalreserve.gov/boarddocs/speeches/2005/20050826/default.htm).

8. Alan Greenspan, "Economic Flexibility" (Speech, National Association for Business Economics Annual Meeting, Chicago, Illinois [via satellite], September 27, 2005) (www.federalreserve.gov/boarddocs/speeches/2005/20050927/default.htm).

9. Alan Greenspan, "The Economic Outlook" (Testimony, Joint Economic Committee, U.S. Congress, June 9, 2005) (www.federalreserve.gov/boarddocs/testimony/2005/200506092/default.htm).

10. Ben S. Bernanke, "Asset-Price 'Bubbles' and Monetary Policy" (Speech, New York Chapter of the National Association for Business Economics, New York, October 15, 2002 (www.federalreserve.gov/boarddocs/speeches/2002/20021015/default.htm).

11. Alan Greenspan, "The Challenge of Central Banking in a Democratic Society" (Speech, Annual Dinner and Francis Boyer Lecture of the American Enterprise Institute for Public Policy Research, Washington, D.C., December 5, 1996) (www.federalreserve.gov/boarddocs/speeches/1996/19961205.htm).

12. Federal Open Market Committee, Federal Open Market Committee Meeting Transcript, September 24, 1996 (www.federalreserve.gov/FOMC/transcripts/1996/19960924Meeting.pdf).

13. Alan Greenspan, "Monetary Policy and the Economic Outlook" (Testimony, Joint Economic Committee, U.S. Congress, April 17, 2002) (www.federalreserve.gov/boarddocs/testimony/2002/20020417/default.htm).

14. You can find the history of booms and busts at the web site of the National Bureau of Economic Research, which is the official dater of recessions (www.nber.org/cycles/cyclesmain.html).

CHAPTER 4   Reading the Federal Reserve

1. Monika Piazzesi and Eric Swanson, "Futures Prices as Risk-Adjusted Forecasts of Monetary Policy," NBER Working Paper No. 10547 (June 2004) (www.nber.org/papers/W10547).

2. Alan S. Blinder and Charles Wyplosz, "Central Bank Talk: Committee Structure and Communication Policy" (Prepared for the session "Central Bank Communication," Allied Social Sciences Association [ASSA] meetings, Philadelphia, January 9, 2005).

3. Federal Reserve Board, *The Federal Reserve System: Purposes & Functions*, Chapter 3: "The Implementation of Monetary Policy," 28 (www.federalreserve.gov/pf/pdf/pf_complete.pdf).

4. Ibid., 45.

5. Ibid., 29.

6. Allan H. Meltzer, *A History of the Federal Reserve*, Volume 1: 1913–1951 (University of Chicago Press, 2003), 699–712.

CHAPTER 5   Prices and the Fed

1. Federal Open Market Committee, Minutes of the Federal Open Market Committee, September 20, 2006 (www.federalreserve.gov/fomc/minutes/20060920.htm).

2. Ben S. Bernanke, "Deflation: Making Sure 'It' Doesn't Happen Here" (Speech, National Economists Club, Washington, D.C., November 21, 2002) (www.federalreserve.gov/boarddocs/speeches/2002/20021121/default.htm).

3. Federal Reserve Press Release, May 6, 2003 (www.federal reserve.gov/boarddocs/press/monetary/2003/20030506/default.htm).

4. Federal Open Market Committee, Minutes of the Federal Open Market Committee, June 24–25, 2003 (www.federal reserve.gov/fomc/minutes/20030625.htm).

5. Federal Reserve Press Release, August 12, 2003 (www.federal reserve.gov/boarddocs/press/monetary/2003/20030812/).

6. Federal Open Market Committee, Minutes of the Federal Open Market Committee, August 12, 2003 (www.federal reserve.gov/fomc/minutes/20030812.htm).

7. Ibid.

CHAPTER 6   McCulley

1. Jonathan Fuerbringer, "During a Bear Market, There's Really No Place like Home," *The New York Times*, August 16, 2001, Business Day, City Edition, Copyright © 2001 The New York Times.

2. Jennifer Ablan, "Recovery Signs Send Rates Soaring," *Barron's*, Current Yield, March 9, 2002, Copyright © 2002 Dow Jones & Company, Inc.

3. Jonathan Lansner, "Interest-Rate Watcher Likes to Take Icon Down a Peg," *Orange County Register*, June 23, 2002, News.

4. Alan S. Blinder and Charles Wyplosz, "Central Bank Talk: Committee Structure and Communication Policy" (Prepared for the session "Central Bank Communication," Allied Social Sciences Association [ASSA] meetings, Philadelphia, January 9, 2005).

5. Jonathan Fuerbringer, "A Bond Master Reflects on Flirting with Disaster," *The New York Times*, February 27, 2000, Money and Business, City Edition. Copyright © 2000 The New York Times.

CHAPTER 7 Speaking Of . . .

1. Adam Smith, *An Inquiry into the Nature and Causes of the Wealth of Nations* (New York: Random House, 1937; orig. pub. 1776), Book IV, Chapter 2, 423.
2. John Maynard Keynes, *The General Theory* (New York: Harbinger paperback edition, Harcourt, Brace & World, 1964; orig. pub. 1936), Chapter 14, 184.
3. Ibid., Chapter 12, 161–162.
4. Herbert Hoover, *The Memoirs of Herbert Hoover*, Volume 3: *The Great Depression 1929–1941* (New York: Macmillan, 1951), Chapter 4, 30.
5. Keynes, *General Theory*, Chapter 12, 150–151.
6. Hyman P. Minsky, "The Financial Instability Hypothesis," Working Paper No. 74, May 1992, Jerome Levy Economics Institute of Bard College (Prepared for *Handbook of Radical Political Economy*, edited by Philip Arestis and Malcolm Sawyer [Aldershot, UK: Edward Elgar, 1993]), 6–8.
7. Ben S. Bernanke, "Some Thoughts on Monetary Policy" (Speech, Japan Society of Monetary Economics, Tokyo, May 31, 2003) (www.federalreserve.gov/boarddocs/speeches/2003/20030531/default.htm).
8. Ibid.
9. Ben S. Bernanke, "Deflation: Making Sure 'It' Doesn't Happen Here" (Speech, National Economists Club, Washington, D.C., November 21, 2002) (www.federalreserve.gov/boarddocs/speeches/2002/20021121/default.htm)
10. Keynes, *General Theory*, Chapter 12, 154–155.

CHAPTER 8 Driving Your Portfolio

1. Jonathan Fuerbringer, "International Investments: The New Landscape," in *The New Rules of Personal Investing*, edited by Allen R. Myerson (New York: Times Books, 2001), 152–183. Copyright © 2001 Times Books.

2. Standard & Poor's, "S&P Emerging Market Indices Methodology, Defining Emerging Markets," August 2006, 2–3 (www2.standardandpoors.com/spf/pdf/index/emdb_methodology.pdf).

3. International Monetary Fund, *Global Financial Stability Report*, Chapter 2: "Global Financial Market Developments," September 2005, 29.

4. International Monetary Fund, *Global Financial Stability Report*, Chapter 1: "Assessing Global Financial Risks," September 2006, 14.

5. International Monetary Fund, *Global Financial Stability Report*, Chapter 3: "Aspects of Global Asset Allocation," September 2005, 76.

6. International Monetary Fund, *Global Financial Stability Report*, Chapter 2: "Global Financial Market Developments," September 2005, 58.

7. International Monetary Fund, *Global Financial Stability Report*, Chapter 3: "Structural Changes in Emerging Sovereign Debt and Implications for Financial Stability," April 2006, 87–88.

8. International Monetary Fund, *Global Financial Stability Report*, Chapter 1: "Assessing Global Financial Risks," September 2006, 23.

9. Ibid., 16.

10. The returns, standard deviations, and Sharpe ratios used in these sample portfolios were calculated by PIMCO.

Following are the "Fed Focus" and "Global Central Bank Focus" columns by Paul McCulley on which a lot of the book is based, listed by chapter. The full columns can be found on PIMCO's web site at www.pimco.com/LeftNav/ContentArchive/Default.htm.

CHAPTER 1 New Steps

"In the Fullness of Time," Fed Focus, January 2000.

CHAPTER 3 What Can Go Wrong

"Twice Blessed," Fed Focus, March 2004.

"If Only Alan Would Shrug," Fed Focus, May 2000.

"Reflexive Disintermediation: Say What? Learning to Live with It," Fed Focus, November 2005.

"Such a Lovely Place," Fed Focus, May 2002.

"Slow and Easy, Baby," Fed Focus, April 2005.

"Eight Tracks Don't Fit in a CD Player," Fed Focus, December 2001.

"Our Currency, but Your Problem," Fed Focus, October 2003.

"Confessions of Optimistic, Principled Populists," Fed Focus, December 2004.

CHAPTER 4 Reading the Federal Reserve

"Reflexive Disintermediation: Say What? Learning to Live with It," Fed Focus, November 2005.

"Fundamentals in Technical Drag Are Still Fundamentals," Fed Focus, May 2005.

"Keeping the Rabbit at Home and the Dog at the Office," Fed Focus, July 2005.

"The Root of All Evil," Global Central Bank Focus, May 2006.

"Shades of Irrational Exuberance," Fed Focus, January 2005.

"My Best Shot," Fed Focus, June 2003.

" 'Uncle,' Uncle Alan, 'Uncle!' " Fed Focus, December 2000.

"Comments before the Money Marketeers Club: Musings on Inflation Targeting," Fed Focus, March 2006.

"Sunshine Is a Great Disinfectant," Fed Focus, September 2003.

"In Democracy We Trust," Fed Focus, August 2004.

"Of Vices and Virtues," Fed Focus, October 2002.

"Moral Hazard Interruptus," Global Central Bank Focus, June 2006.

CHAPTER 5   Prices and the Fed

"I Have Become an Inflation Targeter," Fed Focus, May 2003.

"Comments before the Money Marketeers Club: Musings on Inflation Targeting," Fed Focus, March 2006.

"At Seventeen," Global Central Bank Focus, September 2006.

CHAPTER 6   McCulley

"A Debtor's Blessing," Fed Focus, November 2004.

"My Best Shot," Fed Focus, June 2003.

"Eating Crow With A Dr Pepper Chaser," Fed Focus, April 2002.

"Eight Tracks Don't Fit in a CD Player," Fed Focus, December 2001.

CHAPTER 7   Speaking Of . . .

"Mew Drag," Fed Focus, December 2005.

"Putting Politics in Your Economics," Fed Focus, March 2005.

"In Democracy We Trust," Fed Focus, August 2004.

"Capitalism's Beast of Burden," Fed Focus, January 2001.

"Ben in Tokyo: What He Said There Remains There," Fed Focus, April 2006.

"Fundamentals in Technical Drag Are Still Fundamentals," Fed Focus, May 2005.

"Pyrrhic Victory?" Fed Focus, September 2005.

"The Right Way," Fed Focus, October 2001.

"Is the Price Right?" Fed Focus, January 2006.

Index

About the Authors

Paul McCulley is a money manager at PIMCO, the bond mutual fund powerhouse; an economic forecaster; and an expert on the Federal Reserve. He manages some $20 billion of private and fund portfolios, including the PIMCO Short-Term Fund, which is more than $3 billion. He also oversees PIMCO's liquidity desk, which manages more than $100 billion of money-market instruments. He is an economist and has worked on Wall Street since 1983, including stints at E. F. Hutton & Company; Columbia Savings and Loan Association in Beverly Hills, which he left before it was overwhelmed by its $4 billion of junk bonds in 1991; and UBS Securities, where he set up the firm's economic forecasting unit. Since September of 1999, he has expressed his views on Federal Reserve monetary policy, markets, and economic thought in a column originally called "Fed Focus" and recently renamed "Global Central Bank Focus." He is the son of a Baptist minister and grew up in Verona, Virginia. He received a bachelor's degree in economics from Grinnell College in 1979 and an MBA from Columbia University Graduate School of Business in 1981.

Jonathan Fuerbringer was with *The New York Times* from 1981 to 2005. In New York, he wrote about financial markets, including stocks, bonds, commodities, and currencies; the Federal Reserve and budget surpluses under President Clinton; and budget deficits under the second President Bush. He also wrote a weekly column on markets and investing called "Portfolios, Etc." From Washington, he covered the Federal Reserve as it began its historic fight against inflation in 1979, wrote about economic policy and budget deficits under President Reagan and covered

Capitol Hill. He began his career at the *Boston Globe* and then went to the *Washington Star*, which folded in 1981. He is the son of a journalist, and grew up in suburbs of New York City. He graduated from Harvard College with a B.A. in American history in 1967 and from Columbia Graduate School of Journalism in 1968 with an M.S. in journalism. If he is not writing about financial markets and investing, he can be found at his home outside Arezzo in Italy.